D1137037

HOW TO MAKE A
LIVING
WITH YOUR
WRITING

BOOKS, BLOGGING AND MORE

Joanna Penn

Contents

Yes, it is possible!

We're living in the best time ever to make a living with your writing!

The internet makes it possible to sell to a global audience and use your writing as the way to earn money to fund your lifestyle. If you love to create new things in the world, you can now earn decent money doing it. If you're ready to learn different skills and adapt to a changing environment, this can be a new, exciting phase in your life.

In this book, I'm going to explain exactly how I make a living with my own writing and how you can do it too. I'm going to be realistic and practical with the aim of giving you actionable advice that you can implement for yourself. Each chapter will provide ideas that you can use to research each opportunity further. Sometimes it's just about knowing what's out there in order to set you on the right path.

This is not a get rich quick scheme.

I'm not a Kindle or blogging millionaire. But I will share with you how I make a multi-six-figure income from writing books, blogging and marketing in an ethical manner.

But first, some context: here's a little bit about my own journey.

I did a Masters degree in Theology at the University of Oxford – not the most useful degree! This led to a job in consulting, and I spent the next 13 years implementing Accounts Payable and Banking into large corporates and small/medium companies across Europe and Asia Pacific. I was a cubicle slave and I certainly didn't start out doing creative work.

There were many times when I wondered how I had ended up doing a job that paid well but left me creatively stunted. I enjoyed the pay check, but every couple of years I would resign and try something new.

I started an online travel itinerary website, then a scuba diving charter boat business, then I tried property investment, as well as taking time out to travel. None of my ideas worked out and I had to go back to consulting work every time I ran out of money. I became incredibly frustrated by my seeming incapacity to find meaningful work. By 2006, I knew I had to do something to change my life. I started reading self-help books and decided to write my own book about the search for a job I loved.

That first book changed my life – not because it sold many copies – but because it opened up a new world to me.

I learned about writing books, self-publishing, online marketing, blogging, podcasting and social media. I started selling books, products and services online. I embarked upon a journey that led to me writing both non-fiction and fiction, speaking professionally around the world and finally leaving consulting in September 2011 to become a full-time author entrepreneur. I rewrote that first book as *Career Change* in 2012 and it contains everything I learned about the steps to change your career direction.

My business, The Creative Penn, started off small and I'll admit to a few wobbly moments in the first year, but it has grown in online reach and influence, income and number of intellectual property assets in the last few years. Through the blog, podcast and speaking, I also get to help others realize their dreams of writing and publishing.

This truly is meaningful work, and I'm so much happier. That's ultimately the most important thing. In the last few months, a number of people in our family and friendship circle have died or been sick. These tragic moments bring home the importance of living every day to its fullness.

What do you want to do with your life?

You need to answer that question for yourself, because life is way too short to spend it doing things you hate or that don't bring you alive. If you love to write, I hope this book will help you to make a living from it.

You can also work through the questions in the book with the downloadable Companion Workbook at: www.TheCreativePenn.com/makealiving-download

Plus you can get a free video series at: www.TheCreativePenn.com/freedom

* * *

Disclaimer: I am not a lawyer and this is not legal, contractual or financial advice. It is just my opinion and I can't answer any legal, contractual or financial questions.

How I make a living with my writing

There have been a number of surveys in recent years that report the average income for authors. Most range between US$5,000 and US$30,000 per year.

That's not what I call a living.

In my experience, if you want to make a decent living, you have to develop **multiple streams of income**. That's what we're going to go through in this book, and it's how I run my own business.

As an overview, my multi-six-figure income breaks down as follows:

- **50% - fiction and non-fiction book sales**, including ebooks, print and audiobooks sold on multiple platforms so I am not dependent on one company for income. This is made up of lots of books in lots of formats on lots of platforms, so even if one dips, the others will buoy up sales.

- **25% - affiliate commission** from ethically selling other people's products/services from my blog. I usually receive around twenty different affiliate payments per month.

- **10% - course sales** from my own products sold from my website. Authors have often included teaching as part of their income portfolio and this can be expanded with online tools

- **10% - professional speaking** fees, from multiple companies/events.

- **5% - consulting, podcast sponsorship.**

These income streams separate into two main areas:

A) books

B) blog / platform-related, since I am able to earn from those other income streams purely because I have an audience on TheCreativePenn.com driven by writing articles, making videos and podcasting over the last eight years.

This book is separated into these two main channels. But first, there are some important principles to keep in mind as you read on.

First principles

There are some important first principles to consider before we get into the nitty-gritty of the book. These will frame what we cover in the following chapters.

(1) Think of yourself as an entrepreneur

I know that many writers struggle with 'entrepreneur' because it sounds like a Silicon Valley word that is somehow removed from creating art. But consider it another way.

Entrepreneurs **create value from ideas.**

If you agree with that, then writers are the ultimate entrepreneurs, because we take our ideas and create books, ebooks, print books, audio books, scripts, and lots of other ways of taking words and turning them into value. That value may be giving readers entertainment, information or inspiration, and it creates value for you as the creator in terms of an income.

Once you reframe your own identity as an entrepreneur, you will find it much easier to get your head around some of the ideas in this book. Of course, you'll need to learn new skills, but that's true of anything in life, and entrepreneurs thrive on new challenges!

(2) Focus on creating scalable income

In most standard day jobs, you work for a certain number of hours and you get paid for those hours. If you don't work, you don't get paid or you get sacked at some point for not adhering to your contract. Your work is not scalable, as you're paid once for the hours that you work. And you don't get that time ever again.

With scalable income, you **create once and sell over and over again**.

Let's say you spend a year of your evenings and weekends on writing a book. That time is spent once, but that book can sell one copy, or it can sell 100 copies, 1000 copies, even a million copies. It can also earn money for the life of the author plus 70 years after the author dies, which is the current copyright period. So, your time is spent once but the income from that time can continue for many years.

We're talking about **creating intellectual property assets that will put income in your pocket for years to come**. It might be a small trickle every month at first, but that will increase in time as you add more to your portfolio.

Start thinking about shifting your income streams from being paid by the hour to being paid for scalable assets.

Most of us need to have a balance at the beginning, as we need immediate cash flow to pay the bills, but think about your time as precious when you sit down to work. Is what you're doing scalable?

I changed the balance over a number of years. In 2007, when I started writing books, my scalable income was 0% because I had a day job and only got paid for the hours I worked. I spent nearly four years writing in the evenings and weekends while I worked at my day job, steadily growing my number of books and products, altering my percentage split over time.

In 2017, my scalable income is now around 80%. I still do some non-scalable work e.g. professional speaking and consulting, which provides short term cashflow (we all need that!), but I try to focus most of my time into creating scalable assets.

(3) Develop multiple streams of income

Let's take a little trip back in time to February 2008 when I was working in a large IT department at a mining company in Australia.

The global financial crisis hit and in one single day 400 of us were laid off. Our manager came in to say goodbye with a stack of papers, handed them out and we all scrambled to find new work. At that point in my life, my job was my only source of income, and in one fell swoop, it was all taken away. I decided then and there to never rely on one company for all of my income again.

Nothing is stable, corporations least of all.

Many people had a similar realization back in 2008. It was a wake-up call for developing multiple sources of income and not relying on a job or a company to look after you.

But it's the same principle for making a living with your writing. It's important to make sure that you have more than one source of incoming cash. If you're reliant on one publisher, one self-publishing distributor, one client, one product or one book, at some point, you're likely to find yourself in trouble.

(4) Think global, digital and mobile

Many writers are focused on selling locally, either at a bookstore in their town, or writing for media that people they know have heard of. But we live in a fast-changing world, and global internet penetration is expanding every month. Technology now enables us to sell and market to people all over the world.

If you want to make a living from your writing, then expand your horizons, because your future income is likely to come from the rest of the world, not your local bookstore. A book that will change your perception on this is *Abundance: The Future is Better than you Think* by Peter Diamandis and Steven Kotler. Or check out www. SingularityHub.com.

(5) Decide on your definition of success

This book is about how to make a living with your writing. But the definition of *living* will be very different depending on your situation in life and what you need to meet your monthly outgoings. Consider the following.

- How much is your household income right now?

- How much are your household expenses and monthly outgoings?

- What are you willing to change or sacrifice to alter your situation?

- How much do you really need as a living? For example, many writers move to a cheaper city in order to downsize.

- How long are you willing to wait to make the change?

It's important to consider these questions, because if you don't know what your definition of success is, how will you know if you make it and how will you know how to get there?

Write down your definition of a living and how much you want to earn from your writing in the next year and then the next five years.

Go on – push yourself!

Since we'll be talking about books in particular, you will also need to **decide what you want for your writing career**, as this will determine what you write, how you publish and what you do for marketing.

There are two extreme ends of the author success scale.

At one end is E.L. James with *Fifty Shades of Grey*, who made $95 million in a single year with book sales and movie deals. Her books have sold over 100 million copies. Not many people would say that *Fifty Shades* is great literature – but readers love the books and it sure is making a living!

At the other end is wanting to win the Booker Prize or the Pulitzer or other literary prizes where the aim is critical acclaim as opposed money. Of course, you do get *some* money. The Man Booker Prize winner gets £50,000. That might sound a lot to some people, but it's nothing compared to E.L. James, and it's not much of an annual income if it's taken you five years to write the book.

So you have to consider these two extremes for yourself: **literary success vs. commercial success**, critical acclaim vs. readers buying your books in mass volume and the associated income.

Most authors will say that they want to be somewhere in the middle. They want to write a really good book that critics will like and will also be a commercial success. But that's very hard to do and that's where many writers earning below average incomes sit. Genre fiction sells much better than literary fiction in general, but genre fiction is unlikely to win you a prize, certainly in the main literary fields.

It's really about considering **what's important to you** and about how you're going to measure that success.

Tips on writing and productivity

This is not a writing craft book but it's important to mention productivity – how you actually produce your books – because this is the crux of it. You can't make a living from your writing if you're not actually writing. And while writing may seem easy to some, and it has its fun moments, it's actually really hard work! I think it's the best job in the world (for me) but it's certainly not for everyone.

Here are my tips on getting the words done.

(1) Sort out your routine and writing habits

Every writer is different but every professional writer also has some kind of routine to get the words onto the page. You can call this discipline if you like, but it's better to think of it as a habit. Habits are things you do without having to debate whether to do them or not. Like brushing your teeth, which you likely do at the same time every day without question.

In my first four years of writing books and blogging, I also had a demanding day job as an IT consultant. Because I was drained by the end of the day, I would get up at 5am and write *before* going to work and also set aside a bigger chunk of time to write on the weekends. In the evenings, I worked on my website, podcast and social media, connecting with other authors and building my online platform.

I wrote several non-fiction books and also my first three novels this way.

In many ways, it's easier to write when you have a day job.

Your time is restricted so you have to make the most of the little you have and you're driven to achieve in that period. The financial side is also taken care of so you have less pressure. But of course, you're likely reading this because you want to switch!

I switched to being a full time author entrepreneur in September 2011 and in the first year, it was difficult to find a routine. After 13 years of commuting and office work, it was hard to adapt to working from home alone. I solved this problem by joining a library and taking the train into town with my husband, then working "office hours" and taking lunch or coffee breaks with other author friends, most of whom I met on Twitter.

You'll need to play around with what works for you, but here's what I've found for my own routine:

- I'm a morning person so I need to do creative work in the morning and then do marketing and business admin activities after 2pm. I also write non-fiction or blog posts and articles in the afternoon, then I wind down in the evenings. **Work out when your most creative time is** and use that for first draft creative material.

- Creating can be mentally tiring. Writing fiction in particular can really take it out of you, so **getting enough sleep is critical**. I usually get 8 hours a night and sometimes I'll sleep 10 hours after a big writing day. Our brains pay the bills so we need to look after them.

- I tend to write new words away from my home desk, because I also use that for podcasting, accounting and other things. So **I write in libraries or cafes** and I always plug in my headphones, listen to rain and thunderstorms album on repeat, turn up the volume and start to write.

- **Diarize your time** and make slots for your writing as you would for any other appointment. If you think you don't have enough time, then look at what to eliminate in order to make room. You'll find a way if you really want to write. It's all about where you choose to spend your energy. You get what you focus on.

(2) Get the right tools for the job

We are super lucky as authors because the tools we need are minimal and cheap compared to other businesses. I briefly ran a scuba diving business in New Zealand and the overheads were huge. We had a boat and loads of dive gear, not to mention the cost of fuel, insurance, wages, food etc. These days, all I need are a laptop and an internet connection!

I have a MacBook Pro and I use it for writing as well as making videos, podcasting, email and the usual business admin. Veteran professional author Dean Wesley Smith recommends having a separate computer for writing so you can get into focus mode without distraction, but I've managed this by changing location. However, if you can't escape the addictive pull of the internet during writing sessions, then maybe getting something basic to write on and disabling the internet is a good idea. Turn off your phone as well!

The other tool I'd struggle without is Scrivener software. I use it to plot and (roughly) outline as well as write, organize and manage my books. It's incredibly powerful software and if you want to maximize your usage, I recommend the Learn Scrivener Fast training course which you can find at www.TheCreativePenn.com/scrivener. You can also watch a free video where I talk you through my writing tips as well as how I use Scrivener for fiction and non-fiction at: www.TheCreativePenn.com/writing-tips

(3) Understand first draft writing vs editing and redrafting

Words do not stream from a writer's fingertips perfectly in order, each word exactly as it will be in the final draft. Writers will usually create a first draft, a splurge of words and ideas that definitely will NOT be seen by others. They will then spend time rewriting, editing and polishing until the manuscript is ready for public consumption. I've also found this is true for blog posts and articles as much as books.

Yes, there are some exceptions but understanding this freed me up enough to write books. I recommend you read Anne Lamott's book, *Bird by Bird* where she explains that you have to, "write shitty first drafts." Then clean them up!

Remember, you can't edit a blank page. So just get black on white and work through edits later. Here are some tips for getting that first draft done: www.TheCreativePenn.com/firstdraft

(4) Fill the creative well and then trust emergence

If you want to write for a living, you need to have a consistent flow of ideas that can be used in whatever you're writing next. I still remember when this seemed impossible to me but once you start the flow, I assure you that ideas will never be a problem again. The problem will be turning those ideas into words and finished products.

So how do you start the flow of ideas?

For me, it's all about research – this can be online or through books, but I also like to visit places, immerse myself in new experiences and give synchronicity a chance. I often find things in museums that end up in my books, or I might be at an event and get an idea, or I'll be watching TV or a film and something will spring to mind.

For example, I was watching a documentary on ocean creatures and wondered how biohacking could be used to make human skin more like a shark's. I just wrote that thought down. There's no need to do anything with it right now, so I just log it and trust that I will come back to it another time. Or not. It doesn't matter. But getting used to the process of noticing ideas and writing them down will prime the pump.

Trust your curiosity and write everything down.

I use the Things app on the iPhone which syncs to my Mac and I have a special folder for ideas where I just log a line or two per idea. I have also started to use Evernote. You can use a notebook or any other app, but definitely have some way to note your thoughts down so you can go through them later.

When I write, ideas filter up from my subconscious, often from things I saw or experienced years ago. In my ARKANE thriller *Gates of Hell*, I ended up writing about Safed, a little town in Israel that I visited way back in 1990. It emerged in the story somehow and I wrote from my memories of it, aided by Google, of course!

I don't believe in writer's block. I think it's a symptom of letting the creative well run dry. More about that in my book, *The Successful Author Mindset*. But for now, go fill up your creative well, tune into your curiosity and then come back to the page.

(5) Find your voice by writing lots

Here's a question for you to consider.

If someone writes 10 books, which book will be the best? Number 1 or number 10?

Hopefully the answer is obvious, because practice and experience result in better everything.

But so many writers get obsessed over their first book, spending years writing, editing and polishing it without moving on to the next one. We all have self-doubt, we all suffer from fear of failure, fear of judgment. That never stops, even for the most experienced writers from what I've heard.

The best thing to do is to write that book, then another, then another, then another. Work with a professional editor on every book and learn from the experience. You will improve every time. Read a lot and learn from other writers. Practice technique as you write, focusing on different aspects per book.

And finally, remember to relax into it and have fun! I used to take myself so seriously, but these days, I try to bring joy into my writing. This is not war and peace. No one is going to die (except in your stories, perhaps).

Focus on entertaining, educating or inspiring your readers and just write more.

Tips on mindset

This book mainly focuses on the practical side of making a living, but there are some important mindset considerations as well if you want to be successful. I go into a lot more detail in *The Successful Author Mindset*, so this is just an overview.

(1) Maintain a positive, proactive 'can do' attitude

No one can give you the exact specifications of how to do everything. You can read this book and many others but at some point you have to just get on with it. It's also much easier to learn by doing rather than reading. Play around with the publishing sites, with WordPress, with social media.

Don't take it all so seriously!

Don't be afraid to experiment and take risks. Yes, you will get knocked down. You will fail. But you just have to get up again and give it another go. In this way, you'll develop resilience which is something every writer needs. Because you *will* experience criticism and negativity. It's inevitable.

Here are some examples:

- Comments from your writing group or book group, none of whom are making a living as a writer. "Why are you writing genre fiction?" or "I don't like that character," with no suggestions for improvement.

- Comments from your family, your partner, your friends, your work colleagues. "But you can't write, you've never written anything" or <insert your favorite takedown comment here>.

- 1 star review on Amazon or Goodreads. "This is the worst book I've ever read."

You can't avoid the criticism, you can only try to weather the storms by maintaining a positive attitude.

(2) Keep focused on YOUR definition of success and ignore everyone else's

This is important as you may find yourself off course, chasing something that doesn't fit what you actually want. It's easy to get waylaid into things you don't want or need to do just because people say you have to.

A few years ago, I attended a literary festival and was upset when some authors snubbed me because I was an indie (self-published). I took some of the comments from speakers personally and came away feeling like I was a failure because I didn't have a book deal and I would never speak on stage with my idols.

I could have changed direction and focused on writing more literary books. But then I reassessed my own definition of success. I am more focused on freedom of lifestyle and making a living with my writing, as well as developing direct relationships with readers. The authors on stage mostly had day jobs and only published books every couple of years. They were briefly in the spotlight but they weren't living the life I wanted.

I refocused on my indie writing and publishing and a couple of years later, I ended up speaking at the same festival – as an indie. I've also attracted a literary agent with my self-publishing success.

So, write down your definition of success and pin it near your writing desk!

(3) Find your tribe and embrace social karma

It's important to find a community of authors who will help you through difficult times and who you can learn from. There will always be people ahead of you and behind you, and all of us need to pay it forward and help others as we move up the ladder.

Read blogs and find your online mentors. Read books by other authors, on both craft and business, and for the pleasure of reading. Join a Facebook group with people who have a positive mindset. Surround yourself with those who love writing and get out of toxic discussions quickly.

Join a professional organization like the Alliance of Independent Authors. The Facebook group is super helpful and you'll always get useful answers to your questions. Social media can work for connecting with readers, but it's also brilliant for making friends and connecting with peers around the world. Some of my best friends these days are people I met on Twitter, and now we see each other in real life too.

Social karma is about generosity: sharing other people's blog posts, talking about other people's books and reviewing them on Goodreads. It's about giving what you would like to receive with no expectation of it coming back to you in exactly the same way. This positive energy will keep you enthused and will attract others to you. It's also a happier way to live!

(4) Keep learning all the time and expect change

This book only skims the surface and there's a lot to learn if you want to make a successful living with your writing. The pace of change is only accelerating with new tools and opportunities every week. If you want to keep up, I share a lot of news and stories on Twitter @thecreativepenn and also talk about the bigger things on The Creative Penn podcast. I find audio one of the best ways to stay positive and motivated. By listening and learning from other authors, you will find your own path becomes clearer.

OK, let's get on with the practical stuff! Read on to find out how to make money from books.

Part 1: How to Make Money with Books

1.1 It's not just one book!

This section is all about making money from writing books. We'll look at the rights model, your options for publishing and tips for maximizing income this way.

First, let's talk about the magic of publishing books, because this may change your life and it's super exciting!

This is really important, because so many authors think that when they finish a manuscript, they have just one book to show for it. But actually it is much, much more than that. Once the penny drops on how this business model works, you will understand how you can definitely make a living this way and why publishers have fancy offices in New York and London.

Publishers are not charities.

They don't want to publish books in order to help authors, they want to publish books in order to make money. Yes, most people working within publishing truly love books, but the company itself is a business.

Here's how rights work and how one manuscript can turn into multiple products and multiple streams of income. This is just an overview, as I will go into more detail on how to create each one in the following chapters.

First of all, let's take your finished manuscript and think about **ebook editions**. You can sell ebooks on the biggest stores: Kindle, iBooks, Kobo and Nook. But you can also sell on Smashwords, Scribd, Tolino and lots of other global retailers, with more emerging every day as digital reading spreads.

Then you can have a **print edition**. Print on demand

technology means that you don't have to pay upfront or warehouse and ship physical products anymore. You can use services like Createspace or Ingram Spark to upload files and have your print books available for sale online through Amazon, Barnes & Noble and many other online bookstores. When a customer orders the book, one copy is printed and sent directly to them, and you receive whatever profit margin you set up.

Then you can have an **audio edition**, which you can now commission yourself and do royalty split deals with narrators in some countries.

Now multiply those editions by the number of country markets or territories that you can publish in.

Many authors only sell books in domestic markets, but as an independent author you can sell in 190 countries. So far, I've sold my English language books in 84 countries, and the little trickles start to add up over time.

So you can get started with multiple formats in multiple countries, but then there are other possibilities once you become more established as an author.

You can multiply your rights by language. I currently have ebooks and print books available in German, Italian and Spanish, as well as English.

There are also subsidiary rights, for example, **media, film and TV or stage adaptation**. If you're writing short stories, there might be an **anthology** and then you can have the rights back for a **collection**.

This might sound a little overwhelming, but remember, the point here is to show you that one manuscript can turn into multiple streams of income through the power of intellectual property. If you then write more books, the number of income streams continues to multiply.

Hopefully you're now starting to understand why publishers might want to buy your work!

The next chapters will briefly go through the **pros and cons of your publishing options**, as well as how they may impact your capacity for earning a living with your writing.

1.2 Your publishing options: Traditional publishing

When people think about making a living with their writing, they often assume that it's all about getting a traditional publishing deal because that is the dream and, in many cases, the myth of publishing. We hear stories of the outliers and of course, there are tales of amazing success.

But an article in The Guardian UK in October 2016 stated that the average earnings of professional authors fall below the minimum wage at around £12,500 (approximately US$16,000). And it's often reported that the average book will sell fewer than 500 copies, which of course, is not enough for a sustainable income. Of course, the top 1% of authors, the ones you know by name, are making more than six figures but most are not earning anywhere near that amount.

So let's examine traditional or trade publishing in more detail.

This refers to the established system of getting a book deal, which involves submission to agents over a period of time, usually a number of rejections and then (hopefully) being accepted. Then the agent will submit the manuscript to publishers with usually a number of rejections and then (hopefully) a contract is signed. The book will then go through more edits and eventually be published.

The pros of traditional publishing

Here are the reasons you might choose this route:

1. Prestige, kudos and validation

Most authors suffer from self-doubt and wonder if their work is good enough. If you make it through the process to get an agent and then a publisher, approval by these gatekeepers is usually validation that your work is good enough. Even if the book doesn't sell very well on publication, at least somebody thought it worthwhile. If your definition of success includes a traditional deal because of these reasons, then nothing else will do. Embrace your need for validation and go get an agent. (You'll need a different book for that!)

2. An established professional team to work with

Editors, cover designers, formatters and (possibly) marketing help will be provided by the agent and publisher as part of the contract. Marketing effort is usually related to how much is invested in the project, and marketing for publishing companies is usually to booksellers rather than to consumers. But you should at least get a sales team to take your books to bookstores. Many authors say they "only want to write," which is why they want a publisher to handle the rest of it, but most authors will have to be involved in book marketing however they publish.

3. There are no upfront financial costs, and there's usually some kind of advance against royalties

You don't have to pay anyone to get a traditional publishing deal and if you are asked for money, then it is NOT a traditional publishing deal. It's likely to be a vanity publisher and you should be very careful. The median author advance is currently around £5000 or US$8,000.

Increasingly, there are now deals where the author will take higher royalties and a smaller advance, or no advance at all. Remember also that the advance is against royalties, which are usually 7-25% of net book price. So if you get an advance of $10,000, you then have to earn more than $10,000 out of your royalty rate on book sales before you get any more money.

4. Print distribution to bookstores is easier

This is what traditional publishing excels at and what their model is primarily designed to facilitate. Sales reps go around the stores and make it easy for book buyers to select books they like and pay later on one invoice per publisher minus any returns. Books are usually in the store for a month and only remain if they are perennial sellers.

5. Literary prizes and critical acclaim are more likely through traditional publishing, and many literary prizes aren't even open to indie authors

There have been outliers, e.g. *A Naked Singularity* by Sergio De Le Pava which won the PEN/Robert W Bingham Prize, but it's still rare for self-published authors to even be allowed to enter literary prizes. The Alliance of Independent Authors has a campaign for literary prizes to open up to indies, which is resulting in changes to the industry.

6. Potential to become a brand-name author

There are only a few household name authors in the world: Stephen King, Dan Brown, J.K.Rowling and E.L.James for example. These are the superstar writers. Below them are the A-list, most of whom have been writing for many years, people like Lee Child and Nora Roberts, who are treated very well by traditional publishing and wouldn't see any reason to move. Yes, there's still a chance of becoming a writer of that stature through traditional publishing. It's like a lottery ticket. Definitely worth doing if you want to play the game but the odds are most definitely against you, especially in an era of the 'long tail' and an increasingly fragmented media space.

The cons of traditional publishing

These are the main issues with going the traditional route.

1. Incredibly slow process

Writing and editing will be the same regardless of how you want to publish. But then it might take you a year or two to get an agent. Then it might take a year to get a publishing deal and then it will likely be six months to two and half years before your book is launched. So it's a very, very slow process, which is crazy in a world where you can publish on Amazon and your book can be on sale within four hours and then you can be paid 60 days later.

2. Loss of creative control

You give this up when you sign with a publisher and many publishing contracts will license as many rights as possible. Many authors get titles, covers and marketing campaigns that they're not happy with. A friend of mine, Polly Courtney, famously resigned from her publisher on publication day because she was marketed as chick-lit when she writes gritty novels about social issues. She was angry and upset about losing that creative control. You may also get an editor you don't agree with, especially as many of the more experienced editors move up in the company or are working freelance for more money.

3. Low royalty rates

Royalty rates are a percentage of the sale of the book. They're likely to be net, so all the discounts, returns, marketing costs and overheads are taken off the total before your percentage is calculated. Royalty rates for traditional publishing will usually range between 7% and 25%, with the latter on the unusually generous end. The rates will also differ per format e.g. ebook vs. hardback vs. audio. Royalty reports may come every six months for a specific period of sales and many authors report how difficult they are to understand. They may also not tally with the amount of money that you get in your bank account, so authors who are traditionally published can't really do a cash flow forecast for future income, another reason most need another job.

4. Lack of significant marketing help

Increasingly, authors have to do their own marketing and agents will often seek out authors who have a 'platform' or at least an email list of readers already. If you do want a traditional publishing deal, make sure you ask them about the marketing plan and make sure you get more than just inclusion in a bookstore catalogue and a book blogger tour.

5. Potentially prohibitive contract clauses

There are a few clauses that you need to watch out for. One example is the **agency contract**, something that I have had personal experience with.

A few years ago, I had two New York agencies interested in representing me and I went through their contracts. One of them included a clause where the agency would receive 15% of *everything* I published, regardless of whether they sold the work or not, and that included self-published work because they said that they would build my author brand, so they would be responsible for my success. Obviously I wasn't happy with this because I put a lot of work into my platform and building my own brand, and so I went with the other agency who had a simple clause specifying that they wouldn't receive any sales from my self-published work.

Another big issue is signing contracts where they take **World English rights in all formats. Don't do that** because the publisher is unlikely to actually use all those rights and you'll be unable to use them yourself. *(Unless the money is really worth it, of course!)*

Your job and your agent's job, if you have one, is to retain as many rights as possible when you're doing a deal so that you can exploit them in other ways. For example, you could just sell the US and Canadian rights and then self-publish in the rest of the world, including UK/Commonwealth which is a huge area.

Be careful with formats as well, especially audio books. Many publishers take audio rights as part of a standard book contract and then don't actually end up recording it. You don't want that to happen. Either keep audio rights or specify a length of time the publisher has to exploit them before the rights revert to you.

Look at the **term of the contract and the rights reversion clause.** It used to be that there was an out of print clause, but of course, in these days of print on demand and ebooks, a book never goes out of print. You have to consider when you might get your rights back, because what if this goes really, really badly?

It's like a marriage. You don't plan for it to fail, but sometimes it just doesn't work out.

(And I say that as someone who is very happily married – for the second time!) You want to be able to get out of this relationship if it goes bad, or if the publisher just isn't selling enough of your books and you think you can do a better job.

Once you sign a contract for your book, it essentially belongs to the publisher, and it may belong to the publisher for the life of copyright which is the life of the author plus 70 years after you die. That is a really big deal.

You should also look at the **do not compete clause,** because this may stop you publishing during the term of the contract under the same name, in the same world or with the same characters.

For example, you might sign a three-book deal with one book coming out every year starting in a year's time. So, that's four years in which you may not be allowed to publish anything else under that author name, in that world with those characters. You have to really consider whether the money for the contract is worth it. This is where many authors go a bit crazy, because they think, "I should just take whatever contract I'm offered." Many authors will sign deals because they're grateful that they have been offered anything, but you need to value your writing if you want to make a living with it.

Remember how important your rights are over the long term.

Publishers are not charities. They are not doing you a favor by publishing your book. They are businesses and they want to make money.

If you're looking at a traditional publishing deal, there are two books I recommend that you read:

- *Closing the Deal on Your Terms … Agents, Contracts and Other Considerations* by Kristine Katherine Rusch

- *The Nine Worst Provisions in your Publishing Contract* by David Vandagriff

Both of those books will help you with contract terms. Spend a few dollars on these books and you will save yourself money and heartache along the way.

Put publishing into perspective

Try this little exercise:

- Think of your favorite book

- What is the author's name?

- What is the publisher's name?

Most people will have a favorite book and they'll know the name of the author, but they are unlikely to know the name of the publisher. **Because most readers don't shop by publisher.** Publishers and publishing names and imprints only mean something to authors and those in the industry.

So your publishing choice is more a question of the outcome that you want to achieve and your definition of success. It's not really what the reader thinks about.

The money side of traditional publishing

Authors are paid on a schedule included in the contract and this will usually split the money into different payments. Every contract is different but, for example, this could be one third on signing, one third when the manuscript is accepted and one third on publication. That may be split again between multiple books. Let's be generous and assume $100,000 for a three-book deal.

That sounds like every author's dream, right? But practically, the money might look more like this:

- Agent gets 15% = $15,000

- $85,000 goes to the author over 3 years, split into multiple different payments – some on signing and then payments on acceptance and publication of each book over time - so that could be seven individual payments of approximately $12,000

- Remember you will need to pay income tax, so let's estimate that at 20% = $2400 leaving $9600 that you'll get a couple of times a year. Is that enough money for you to live on? Suddenly the six-figure deal for three books is not so attractive.

This is just one example, and every contract will, of course, be different. If you are offered a contract, work out how the payment schedule will really work and don't be overawed by the initial figures.

If you want to make a living with your writing, you need

to understand how the cash flow will work and what dates money will come in.

Would I take a traditional publishing deal?

Absolutely. For the right project and for the right terms and conditions.

I have an agent who is actively working on foreign rights sales – in languages other than English. I'm also keen to exploit film, TV, gaming and other subsidiary rights. I'd also take a deal in English for print format only, for sure, and I'll consider every decent offer for other rights. After all, I can always write more books!

But personally, I choose not to spend my energy chasing these perfect deals. I choose to get my books out into readers' hands as soon as possible and take the cash sooner rather than later, earning for the long term. I'm primarily an indie author, so let's now look at the changes in the publishing industry followed by the pros and cons of self-publishing.

1.3 Changes in the publishing industry

The publishing industry is undergoing a lot of change, with digital disruption shifting the landscape as it did in the music industry a few years back. These changes mean uncertainty and fear for many, but creators who are willing to embrace the new model can do amazingly well. Here are just some of the exciting developments.

Shift in consumer purchasing and reading behavior

In January 2017, a panel at Digital Book World conference reported that:

- "When we look at consumer book buying as a whole, close to 45 percent of *all* books purchased in the US in 2016 were digital."

- In adult fiction, sales in the US are nearly 71 percent digital

- 30 percent of all US adult fiction book purchases are by self-published authors

Ebook sales are also starting to rise in countries other than just the US, UK, Canada and Australia because of the spread of faster internet connections and the use of tablets and cellphones for reading. If you consider that most people in the world don't live near a physical bookshop, purchasing via cellphone will only increase over time.

People will always want education, inspiration and entertainment and they will increasingly get it via their phone.

Sub-Saharan Africa, as well as South American and Asian countries are skipping desktop computers and laptops and moving into the internet age on phones. Those are exciting new markets for writers!

There's also a demographic shift into cities and smaller living spaces, and a trend towards owning less stuff which will increase digital purchases. For example, many people listen to music streaming from the cloud, rather than owning a CD. The same is happening with books through membership programs like Kindle Unlimited and Audible.

Another interesting thing about digital markets is the twin poles of the younger digital natives, those who have grown up with the internet, and the aging population. One of the biggest markets for e-readers is the over 60s because you can change the font size or use Whispersync to listen to books. Just a few years ago, you could only get a small number of large print books and audiobooks in the form of tapes from libraries. Being able to change font size and listen on digital devices has opened up a whole new world of reading for the Boomer generation. The advance of in-home technology like Amazon Echo and Google Home may also increase the number of audiobooks consumed in coming years.

So what about print?

In March 2015, The Bookseller reported that *online* print book purchasing overtook *in-store* print purchasing. That means more people are buying print online than they're buying print in stores, which puts independent authors on a par with traditionally published authors. I have print books for sale online and they have the same chance of being discovered as any other author's books.

The indie movement and how it changes things

The word indie stands for independent, and we're at a point in the world right now where being an indie is pretty cool. If you think of indie musicians or indie film-makers, what words spring to mind?

More original.

More creative. More authentic and edgy.

Separate from the massive labels that treat artists badly.

More character driven, rather than Hollywood blockbuster.

In many creative industries, it's almost preferable to be indie than to be linked with the mega conglomerates that are tied into media companies with dubious interests.

Consider your own purchasing behavior.

- Do you buy indie music and watch indie films?

- Do you drink small batch beer brewed locally by artisan brewers? Or buy cupcakes or artisan bread directly from the baker?

- Do you buy vegetables at your local farmers' market instead of the supermarket chain?

- Do you buy art and craft gift items from NotOnThe-HighStreet or Etsy?

- Have you supported a creative project on Kickstarter or Patreon?

The general public are becoming more and more likely to buy from artists directly and they want to support creative projects and creative people. Even education is heading this way, with the rise of online learning sites full of individuals creating courses on all kinds of topics.

So, we're in a culture where the creator is increasingly valued and that's extremely exciting. So let's talk about how you can take advantage of this shift by considering going indie.

1.4 Your publishing options: Becoming an indie author

There's a difference between self-publishing and becoming a professional indie author.

The term self-publishing implies doing everything yourself and doing it more as a hobby. There's certainly nothing wrong with this and it's wonderful to create books in the world for the love of creation. I self-publish photo books for my own pleasure, I helped my 9-year-old niece self-publish her first book and I helped my Dad self-publish a thriller for his 65th birthday.

But I use the term independent author, or indie author, for myself. I work with top freelance professionals to create a quality product and this is a business for me, not just a hobby. Of course, many professional indie authors start out self-publishing and transition over time. We all have to start somewhere!

The pros of being an indie author

1. Total creative control over content and design

Many authors who were traditionally published and are now indies talk about how painful it was to have a cover or title they hated, or to have editorial choices imposed on them that they didn't agree with but were insisted upon. As an indie, you can work with freelancers of your choice and you can choose the ultimate look and feel of your product.

Now, that can be a pro or a con depending on how the book ends up, but as an indie, you can also change it, as I have done by re-titling and re-covering my first three books. You just upload another file.

This start-up mentality, that mistakes are how we learn and 'failure' is just a step along the way, makes publishing easier for indies.

2. Empowerment

I attended a literary festival recently and talked to a number of traditionally published authors. I was shocked at how insecure they were and how beaten down by the negativity of the publishing process. They really didn't see themselves as being able to make a decision alone or take action to improve their lot, despite the fact that THEY are the creatives, the storytellers, the brilliant ones.

Compare that to indies, who in general are a happy bunch, as reported by publishing industry researcher Alison Baverstock. It's not surprising when you consider the research on 'locus of control.' The Journal of Personality and Social Psychology reported that the number one contributor to happiness is autonomy, "the feeling that your life – its activities and habits – are under your control."

After signing a contract, traditionally published authors have pretty much zero control – over pricing, timing of publication, marketing, sometimes over the cover, the title and even the words themselves. Plenty of authors are told to change their stories to fit what a publisher wants.

Compare that to the empowerment of the indie author who can learn new skills, work with professionals, make mistakes and learn from them, earn money directly and interact with customers.

Yes, it's hard work, but it's certainly empowering! The positive energy involved in being an indie can propel you much further, much faster than waiting in line for your turn.

Stop asking permission. You don't need it.

Stop waiting to be chosen. Choose yourself.

3. Faster time to market

You still have to spend the same amount of time writing and editing. But once you're ready to publish, you can upload your files to Amazon, Kobo, iBooks, Draft2Digital and any other stores. **Your ebook is usually for sale within 8-72 hours**. You're paid 60 days after the end of the month of sale.

If you're doing print on demand, you can get your book up within 24 hours if you approve the formatting online. Or, you can order a copy and it might take a couple of weeks, but essentially, it's incredibly fast to get your book up for sale. This certainly suits my personality, as once I'm done with a book, I want it out there and selling! I don't want to sit on it for several years while it shuttles around the publishing eco-system.

4. Higher royalties

If you price your book between $2.99 and $9.99 on Amazon, you can get a 70% royalty and there is no cap on the other retailers like Kobo and iBooks. Traditional royalty rates usually fit in the 7-25% bracket, averaging 10%. It's clear that you need to sell far fewer books in order to make the same amount of money with self-publishing.

But **it's not a get rich quick scheme**. That's really important to know. You can't guarantee that you're going to make as many sales as you would've done with a traditional publisher, or indeed, any sales at all. That is more to do with genre, investment in marketing and sometimes, pure luck by hitting the zeitgeist at the right time.

An author can't build a business on luck – but they can learn about marketing, and authors have to do that these days, regardless of how they publish.

5. Sell by any means in any global market, as you retain the rights

My books have now sold in 84 countries and they are for sale in 190. I love to look at my sales map to see which new countries I've sold to in the last month. I particularly enjoy selling in countries like Burkina Faso or Namibia in sub-Saharan Africa because I went to school in Malawi (no books sold there yet, though!)

Yes, these sales are a trickle right now, but in the next few years, cell phone penetration will increase and internet access will become globally pervasive.

Two years ago, I was only selling books in the US, UK, Australia and Canada. But pretty much every month, another tiny income stream starts up. This is for books in English by the way – we're so lucky that English is the most international language.

Many traditionally published authors have sold World English rights for all formats and yet have barely sold outside the usual country markets because their books aren't even available in most places in the world. Many have also sold audiobook rights, but the books have not been produced.

If you're in this situation, revisit your contract. What do you hold the rights for? You can self-publish in countries where you haven't licensed the rights, so why not get on with it!

6. Niche books can reach a specific audience

Publishing houses have an expectation of a certain number of sales, so if you're writing a niche book on a particular type of organic tomato, for example, then you might find the market is too small for a major publisher.

But the market size may well be enough to satisfy your own definition of success. You can price as you like, as chances are that your book will appeal to a very particular reader who might pay higher prices.

7. Use it to get into the publishing game

These days, if you self-publish and do well, agents and publishers will come to you. You don't have to beg and plead for attention. The power balance is reversed and the empowered indie can get a much better deal than a first-time author with no evidence of sales.

Just look at the traditional publishing deals that Hugh Howey, Bella Andre, Jasinda Wilder, Meredith Wild and A.G.Riddle have done for both print books and movie/TV deals. So if you want a traditional deal, you could skip the slush pile and serve your apprenticeship as an indie.

The cons of being an indie author

So there's the positive side, but what about the negatives?

1. You need to do it all yourself or find suitable professionals to help

As with any new skill, going indie is a steep learning curve. You still have to do the writing and marketing, but you also have to do the publishing. You have to find an editor and a cover designer to work with, decide on the title, get your work formatted into ebook, print and any other format you want, and find suitable professionals to help. This isn't such a big deal as we all share with each other online and you can join The Alliance of Independent Authors which vets service providers.

But you do have to decide on your definition of success and understand that **you need to run all aspects of the business if you want to go the pro indie route**.

For many people, this is a negative, because they just don't have the time to do everything or they don't enjoy doing it. **I'm lucky because I love being an entrepreneur**. I love all aspects of what I do – from idea generation to creating words on the page, to the technical side of things around formatting and everything in between. After many years, I've found the perfect work for me. If you can manage a project or you could learn to, then you'll likely enjoy it too. But this life is certainly not for everyone.

2. There's no prestige, kudos or validation by the industry

The stigma lessens every day, but if your definition of success is bound up with what other authors, agents and publishers think of you, then indie might not be best for you.

Of course, if you only care about readers, then indie is a great option.

3. You need a budget upfront if you want a professional result

These days, you're likely to spend on professional editing before submitting to an agent anyway, or at least be spending on books and courses for writers. Everyone spends money on their hobby, so whether you're knitting or writing or mountain biking, most people are happy to spend money they never get back on something they love.

However, if like me, you're intending to make a living from this, then yes, you need to invest money in creating assets for the business with the intention of getting it back in multiple streams of income. Either way, you will need a budget upfront if you want to be a pro indie.

4. It's difficult to get print distribution in bookstores

It's certainly not impossible and if you care about print distribution then look at the options with Ingram Spark. Also check out the Opening Up to Indie Authors campaign by the Alliance of Independent Authors.

But you're much more likely to get bookstore distribution with a traditional publisher, as that's essentially their business model and has been for a long time. They are experts at printing and distributing physical product. My personal choice is to use print on demand through Createspace and Ingram Spark, so my print books are available on all online bookstores and in catalogues that libraries and bookstores order from.

5. Most literary prizes don't accept indie books and most literary critics for mainstream media won't review them

If your definition of success is literary and critical acclaim, you're probably better off going the traditional route. Again, the Opening Up to Indie Authors campaign is looking to address this over time.

The hybrid model: It's not an either/or choice anymore

The industry has changed and many authors now take a hybrid approach to publishing. They will make the decision per book per series and by particular rights, using the indie model for some things and taking traditional deals for others. This empowers the author to make decisions and choose the best possible route for each project. After all, **a career isn't built on one book**.

For example, Hugh Howey sold his print rights for *Wool* and did a number of foreign rights deals, as did indie author J.A.Konrath. Jasinda Wilder sold several new books to traditional publishers while continuing to self-publish another series. A.G.Riddle sold his film rights and kept his World English ebook rights as an indie. I have a German language deal with a traditional publisher and a literary agent who is handling other foreign rights sales.

The important thing is that you, the creator, are empowered to choose per project how you would like to progress.

Other publishing options

I've used the two extreme ends of the publishing spectrum as examples but these days, there are many more options for authors. This downloadable chart by Jane Friedman gives a wider view of the options available: www.TheCreativePenn.com/publishingpaths

There are new companies springing up every day – some of which are offering a good deal and some which are just sharks who may well take your money and leave you disappointed. Many of the biggest 'author services' companies are run by Author Solutions, once owned by Penguin Random House, so it is author beware.

Do your due diligence and get testimonials from authors who are happy to recommend a service before you sign anything.

How do you evaluate author services options?

My basic rule is: How does the company make their money?

Traditional publishers should pay you an advance against royalties, so you get the money first and then they make money back as your books sell.

Going completely DIY, as I do, means that you can publish for free *(yes, $0)* on all the direct retailers and they take a percentage of the royalty. **They only make money when you make money.**

If you go indie, you'll need to pay for editing and cover design upfront. But these prices shouldn't break the bank and you should use professionals that other authors have recommended.

If you want to use services that charge for other things, then please check the following resources:

- Watchdog Service Ratings by the Alliance of Independent Authors:

  www.TheCreativePenn.com/watchdog

- Choosing a self-publishing service by the Alliance of Independent Authors, available on all online bookstores. Written by authors and for authors so you get unbiased advice.

Need more help with going indie?

Check out the following resources:

- My own *Author 2.0 Blueprint* ebook and video series available at www.TheCreativePenn.com/blueprint

- My round-up of publishing articles, including how to self-publish an ebook, print book and audiobook: www.TheCreativePenn.com/publishing

- The Alliance of Independent Authors – a brilliant organization for authors who want to professionally self-publish. Members get ebooks and other resources on self-publishing, plus there is a lively Facebook group and a monthly salon where I answer questions alongside Orna Ross, the founder of the Alliance.

1.5 How to self-publish an ebook

If you want to self-publish an ebook, here are the basic steps and my own process for reference. This may look complicated if you're trying it for the first time, but like any skill, it gets easier every time you do it.

The actual process of publishing barely takes any time at all after you've done a couple of books. It's the writing and marketing that take the most time, and that is true however you get your book into the world.

Before you publish

There are a few things you'll need to have in place before you click publish.

Yes, you need a great book!

A professional editor can help with this and I am a huge advocate of spending money and effort on this step in order to have a quality result. Here's my list of editors if you need one: www.TheCreativePenn.com/editors

A title that entices readers

For non-fiction books, you want to use titles that contain the keywords people are actually searching for. For example, I changed the title of my first book to *Career Change* because people were searching for those words. You can research this by typing ideas into the Amazon search bar and seeing what the dropdown contains. The keyword phrases displayed there are the most popular searches.

For fiction, it's more about resonating with your genre and giving an impression of your book, which is much more difficult! You can change book titles, but it is difficult, as I found when I re-titled my first three novels.

A brilliant cover

Spend some time looking at the top selling books in the category you are aiming for on Amazon. Take some screen prints and then work with a book cover designer to create a fantastic cover. You can find my list of designers at www. TheCreativePenn.com/bookcoverdesign.

This is a critical step as your book cover is an important piece of your book marketing. You can also change your cover later as many of us do. Traditional publishers change covers every few years to reinvigorate sales and it's definitely worth doing the same, especially if you have older books.

If you have existing contracts for your books, and /or you have been published in the past, check that you have the rights to the cover before you self-publish existing work. It's unlikely that you do and you'll need a new one.

Write your sales description

This is an art and one that we are all trying to improve!

Your aim is to entice the reader to download a sample or buy. There are many aspects to a good sales description and one way to get into the mood for writing one is to look at 10-15 top selling books in your genre.

Copy out the sales descriptions for each. What do you like? What resonates? What words do they use? Model your own on those. Check out Libbie Hawker's book, *Gotta Read It: 5 Simple Steps to a Fiction Pitch That Sells*, or listen to this interview with Bryan Cohen on writing sales descriptions: www.TheCreativePenn.com/salesblurb

It's much easier for non-fiction. You have to demonstrate that you will answer the reader's question or solve their problem in the book. You can also include your table of contents to show them what's inside. Feel free to include review quotes from other authors and reviewers, but it's not required.

Format your ebook

You need to have a mobi file for Kindle and an ePub file for the other platforms but don't let technicalities put you off. There are a number of options for ebook formatting.

- **Load Word documents** into the various sites e.g. Draft2Digital and let them auto-format your files. This is really only good for plain text and you won't be able to fix up any formatting you don't like.

- **Do it yourself** using Vellum ebook formatting software. This is what I use now as it creates gorgeous ebooks, but it is Mac only. You can find it at: www.TheCreativePenn.com/vellum

- **Pay a professional formatter**. There are lots of professional formatters out there now and some offer print formatting bundled with the ebook. Here's my list: www.TheCreativePenn.com/formatting. You can also ask other authors for recommendations or use the Alliance of Independent Authors Partner member directory.

Some authors don't want to mess around with ebook files. I used to feel like that too, but seriously, if you're publishing a lot, then you will want to have a hand in the process. It will save you loads of money if you're doing this for the long term because most of us update ebooks regularly with new back matter or to fix outdated content.

Publish your ebook

Again, there are a number of options:

Go direct to the retailers

For the best royalty rates, ease of control, speed of changes and enhanced metadata, it's a good idea to publish direct to the retailers, all of which are free.

I use Amazon KDP for Kindle, Kobo Writing Life and iTunes Connect for iBooks.

Use an aggregator like Draft2Digital or Smashwords

You can use one of these sites to distribute to all of the stores, which will cut down on the number of platforms you have to monitor and make changes to. You can also use them for other stores.

I use Draft2Digital to get my books onto other stores, including Nook (although you can use NookPress.com).

During the publishing process, you'll need to:

Choose your categories

Categories are the genres and sub-genres that you will find on the online bookstores, for example, Romance > Historical, or Thriller > Conspiracy.

You assign these to your book when you self-publish and your choices will be critical for discoverability. Spend some time deciding on the best ones for your book.

Think about how people shop on the online book stores or on devices. They will usually drill down into the sub-category that they like to read, for example, I like to surf Thrillers as well as Action Adventure, and in non-fiction I will always check out the latest books in Entrepreneurship and Business. Those count as categories and they can be quite granular.

You can choose to apply two or three categories to your book on most online stores, but a lot more on Apple if you publish direct. Just log onto whichever store you're publishing on and check the dropdown for categories to see your options. For more on categories, check out this interview with Nick Stephenson: www.TheCreativePenn.com/nick.

Choose your keywords

These are words or phrases that can be used to describe your book, but also that customers might use to search. For example, 'career change' is a keyword phrase that I used as a book title as well as a keyword. 'Supernatural thriller series' would be a keyword phrase for my fiction.

Keywords are another mechanism that will help your book be discovered on the stores. They can help you to rank for certain search terms as well as get you into more granular browse categories on Amazon. So for example, my books rank in Conspiracy Thriller, which isn't available in the category field – it can only be chosen through using the keyword phrase 'conspiracy thriller.' As mentioned in the title section above, you can use the Amazon search bar drop down to find appropriate search terms. For more on keywords, check out this article: www.TheCreativePenn.com/keywords

Choose the territories to publish in

If you are self-publishing and you haven't signed a contract for any rights, you can just choose ALL. If you have sold some of your rights, you can still self-publish in other territories. For example, many authors who have sold in the US and Canada could still self-publish in the UK and the rest of the world.

It's really important to think about this, because if you want to make a living with your writing, you want to be publishing in all of these different territories and maximizing your distribution.

Choose your price

There are many debates over pricing and the best advice is not to get too upset about this when you only have a couple of books. Your main focus should be getting initial readers, which may mean pricing for free or cheap so people will take a risk on a new, unknown author.

Once you have a few books, you can price at various levels. For example, I have free books, full-length fiction at $4.99 and novellas at $2.99. My non fiction is higher at $4.99 - $9.99 and I have some boxsets which range from $6.99 to $19.99. Prices over $9.99 aren't recommended on Amazon, as the royalty rate drops but for Apple and Kobo, you can go higher and still receive the top royalty rate. The readers there are often more used to paying higher prices.

A couple more useful points:

Many of the platforms now use a **Series field** to group books together. Make sure that you spell the series exactly the same on every book so that they are correctly linked together. This is critical for the various algorithms to recommend the books as a series. And if you're not writing a series, why not?! It's the best way to make more money as an author.

You can also use **pre-orders** on the retailers, which each have varying guidelines. This is useful if you have a series and you know more books are coming. You can drive sales over a longer period rather than waiting until launch week and then trying to get everyone's attention.

How does the money work?

The percentage royalty differs per retailer and also per region, as well as whether you're in Amazon's exclusive KDP Select program. You can read about the pros and cons of exclusivity here: www.TheCreativePenn.com/exclusive. The range is usually 35%-70% of the net price which you set yourself as a self-published author. You will generally receive payment 60 days after the month of sale so at the end of May, I will receive royalties from March sales. Some retailers pay using PayPal monthly and some quarterly. I can see reports at any time on all the main retailers about my sales so I can forecast my cash flow.

1.6 How to self-publish a print book

Of course you want a print book. You want to hold it in your hand and say, "I made this." If you're like me, you also want to create a 'vanity shelf' over time with all your books on it! And why not, it's a big achievement.

Many readers still read only print books and so it's a slice of the market you want to be able to reach. In March 2015, The Bookseller reported that online print sales had overtaken in-store print sales, so having a print book for sale online can still be effective. It's also good to have print for talks, marketing and giveaways, otherwise some people don't consider you a 'real' author. Silly perhaps, but still surprisingly common.

It's also good for **comparison pricing**. Look at a book sales page on Amazon and if there's an ebook as well as a print book, you'll see a 'saving.' The customer then considers the ebook price to be a good deal. So purely having a print book for comparison pricing is a good reason to do it. This is why I even do print for my short novellas.

There are two main options for publishing print books:

Print on demand:

You upload up your interior and cover files to one of the print on demand (POD) service companies.

When a book is ordered, one copy is printed and sent directly to the customer. No paying upfront for print copies. No holding stock. No post office runs. You just get the profit after the sale. I highly recommend this option for most people as there is very little risk and you can buy a few of your own copies for giveaways, marketing and ego reasons. This is what I do and I'm very happy with it.

Short print run:

This option involves working with a partnership publisher or just a printer and getting a certain number of copies printed before distribution or purchase by customers. You will need to pay for these upfront before you sell them, so it will mean a financial outlay, potentially a considerable one.

This option is only recommended if you have a distribution method in place, e.g. you are a speaker and sell books at the back of the room, or if you have guaranteed sales. I did a short run once – I lost money and the books ended up in the landfill – so please be careful and do your sums if you're going this route. If you want to do a short print run, remember to factor in shipping, since books are heavy and this can add considerable cost.

Before publishing

You will need to have a formatted interior and a book cover ready before you publish. You'll need to decide the size of the print book and either make the files yourself or pay a professional formatter to do this for you.

Your interior formatting options include:

- Use the **free templates** available at the POD companies. Just download the templates for the size you want and complete them.

- For interior files, use the reasonably priced and very professional Book Design Templates:
  www.TheCreativePenn.com/templates

- **Pay a professional formatter**. Here's my list of formatters: www.TheCreativePenn.com/formatting. You can also search for them online or ask other indie authors for their recommendations.

Recommended Print On Demand companies

There are two main options for print on demand, both recommended by many authors.

Createspace:

This is Amazon's own print on demand company. It has a simple 'wizard' process, downloadable templates and online help along the way.

Once you've uploaded your files, you'll be given the cost of the book and then you can add the profit you want to make. You can then proof online or order a copy to check that it's OK before approving for sale in the store. It's free to publish. The only charge is for the proof copy and then you're paid per sale.

The extended distribution option means that your book will be available at online stores around the world.

One little tip, if you are ordering your own books from Amazon regularly, you can get free shipping with Amazon Prime.

In late 2016, Amazon added a print option to the KDP Dashboard, where you used to only publish ebooks. So it's possible that there will be a consolidation in this option as time goes on.

IngramSpark:

If you want to have your books available in physical bookstores and libraries, then Spark is a better option than Createspace. You'll still have to get the various places to order the books, but retailers are more likely to stock books that come through Ingram.

There are some charges depending on what you're doing with your books so you have to decide how print fits into *your* definition of success. The main thing to remember if you want to sell in stores is to ensure that you factor in discounts and returns, which can severely impact profitability. Many professional indies use Createspace for Amazon and then use IngramSpark for the extended distribution option to bookstores.

A word on ISBNs

Many indies consider ISBNs to be important and they certainly are if you want to sell physical books in bookstores or distribute to libraries. They are essential for store ordering systems to track books.

But you don't need ISBNs to make a living with your writing, so it is a personal decision. You can get started without them and use them once your author business grows, as I did.

How does the money work for print on demand?

You set the profit you want to make per book and you can see reports of sales online at any time. You'll be paid by direct deposit or check (dependent on your country) at the end of the month following the month of sale.

1.7 How to self-publish an audiobook

The market for audiobooks is incredibly exciting and there are some big technology developments in recent years that will continue to boost the growth of audio.

Streaming audio in cellphone apps means that it's easier than ever to buy and consume audiobooks and podcasts. Google Auto and Apple Carplay brought streaming audio to cars in 2016 boosting commuter listening.

The Amazon Echo and Google Home brought it into living rooms, syncing with mobile devices. Whispersync technology means that you can be reading on your phone or device at breakfast, then get in your car and continue listening where you stopped reading, and when you get home, cook dinner while listening on your Echo, all without losing your place. Amazon also bundles audiobooks with ebooks, and if a customer owns an ebook version, the audiobook is cheaper.

In addition, the number of audiobooks available right now is considerably smaller than print or ebooks, so you have more of a chance of standing out. Most traditionally published authors have signed away audiobook rights and many of those will never be turned into audio, so indies have the advantage of a faster response to this growing market.

Use ACX to go indie for audio

ACX.com is the Audiobook Creation Exchange, where authors and rights holders can collaborate with narrators and producers to essentially self-publish audiobooks. It's an Amazon company and your book will be for sale on Amazon, Audible and iTunes.

At the time of writing, ACX.com is only available to authors in the US and UK, but hopefully they will be expanding to other territories over time. There are ways to do audio *without* ACX but they are more difficult.

Check out *Making Tracks: A Writer's Guide to Audiobooks and How to Produce Them* by J.Daniel Sawyer if you want to find out more. If you are in the US or UK, read on.

The process works as follows:

The rights holder/author logs into ACX and claims their book.

You can search with the Amazon ASIN, the number that Amazon assigns to every book on the store. You have to legally own the rights to do this, for example, if you're an indie who hasn't signed a contract for the book or a traditionally published author who didn't sell the audio rights.

Enter in extra details about the book relevant for narrators

For example, what type of voice would be best? An older African-American male vs. young adult female would be two extremes. You also add in information about reviews and sales, which is particularly important if you want to attract an experienced narrator.

Decide on the contract

The options are:

a) pay the narrator an amount per final audio hour and you retain the entire royalty

b) do a 50:50% royalty split with a narrator with no money upfront

c) record the audio separately, either yourself or with an external narrator, then upload and retain the entire royalty

Decide on whether you will go exclusive to ACX

If you go exclusive, you will get higher royalties but you won't be able to sell outside the channels of Amazon, Audible and iTunes.

As audiobooks continue to grow as a format, it's likely that other options will emerge for indies through various distributors as they have done for ebooks.

Upload an excerpt from your book for narrators to audition with

Narrators will be alerted to your book and some will audition for you. When auditions come in, you can decide whether or not the narrator is what you're looking for.

You can decline auditions and give feedback if you want. If you're not getting any narrators auditioning, it's likely to be because your book doesn't have enough reviews or sales on it. You can also find narrators through your author contacts and go looking for them instead of passively waiting. I actively found two of my narrators through recommendations from friends, and another found me through ACX.

When you find the right narrator, accept the audition, and then decide on dates for production

You'll need to QA the files, listening and checking the words as well as any issues. I trust my narrators as professionals and I consider the audiobook to be an adaptation, so I only correct obvious pronunciation issues which usually stem from British vs. American pronunciation.

Once the files are QA'd, the audiobook will go live. You will receive some promo codes from ACX so you can get some early reviews on it and then sales should start.

The money side of audio

If you do a royalty split deal with a narrator, there is no money paid upfront and you just split the royalties between you. ACX do this for you so the money is deposited into your bank account every month. Personally, I think this is amazing and in the last year, this has been a fantastic new income stream for me and many other authors.

You can also pay narrators upfront, which will cost several hundred dollars per finished audio hour. You can even hire a studio and narrate the book yourself, as I did for my book, *Business for Authors: How to be an Author Entrepreneur.* Studio costs and audio production help will vary in cost. Most authors with decent sales will cover these upfront costs within the first year, and future sales will be profit. If you retain the rights, then this can be a significant income stream over the long-term.

More help with audio:

It sounds like it's complicated but it's not really, and much easier to do than to write about! If you want to get more details, check out the resources at: www.TheCreativePenn.com/audiobooks

1.8 How to actually make money with books

I'm assuming that you're reading this book because success for you is at least partly defined by sales and income. So, in this section we'll go through how to actually make money from books.

(1) Write more books

This might be obvious, but it's amazing how many authors assume that they can make a good living from just a couple, or even just one book.

But look at every other business out there.

Does any retailer base their business on a small number of products? Does any publisher base their income on just a couple of books?

If you look at the top earning authors in the world, they generally have huge numbers of books and they've been writing for the long term. Many write multiple books a year. If you love writing, then this shouldn't be an issue for you. This will be the fun part, and here's some more good news. **The more books you have, the LESS you have to market them** because you'll have an audience ready and waiting, critical mass on the digital shelves and multiple streams of income.

If you have twenty books, and each book only sells a couple of copies a day, then you're still going to make better money over time than someone with just one book. One book with a great launch might have a spike of sales initially but over time the numbers will shrink, unless another book comes along to boost the signal.

And, of course, as you write more books, you will also become a better writer.

(2) Write books that people want to buy: by genre or category

It doesn't matter how much marketing you do. If you write in a genre/category that doesn't sell, then you won't be able to make a living with your writing.

Harsh, I know. But true.

Of course, you should write the book of your heart. I certainly did with my first book and also a couple of my novels. That's important for your creative integrity. But if you're spending years writing poetry and literary short stories, don't complain if you can't make a living from your writing. Those are for love, not necessarily money, and we all need both!

If you want to know what people are buying, take a look at the top-selling books on Amazon.

Or short cut the process and go check the data on AuthorEarnings.com which shows that 70% of the top 200,000 ebooks are genre fiction, which include romance, mystery/ thriller, sci-fi and fantasy.

How can you write at the intersection of what people love to read and what you love to write? That's the key.

I read a lot in multiple genres, including poetry and literary fiction. But when I was miserable in my day job, I would read thrillers to escape the misery of the day. It was the way I could forget my own life for a while and live vicariously somewhere else. That's what books are for many people. So I write those kind of thrillers now, because I love to read them, and so do many other people. They're also a lot of fun to write. Romance is a better selling genre but I don't read romance, so I won't be writing it. You need to immerse yourself in the genre in order to write it well. You can't fool hardcore readers!

Spend some time looking at the sub-genres and how they are structured.

I know many writers hate 'boxes,' but you have to choose two sub-categories when you self-publish a book and your agent will want to know what you're writing if you want a traditional deal. You need to know who your **comparison authors** are and this will help you to investigate the genres and discover what sells better.

For example, I write books that can sit within Supernatural Thriller, Conspiracy Thriller and Action Adventure. My books don't fit within Medical Thriller or Espionage. Literary fiction is also a genre and there are many sub-genres within the category these days.

Check the rankings of the top books per sub-genre to work out which ones are selling best. Have a look at the covers and the titles, as well as the sales descriptions. What are the images used? What are the expectations of the audience for these types of books? What do the top-selling books have in common? How does your book measure up and what can you do to improve it?

(3) Write books that people want to buy: by search term

People want a book for entertainment, inspiration or information. If you're not a brand-name author already, your non-fiction book is more likely to be discovered if it answers someone's question or helps them solve a problem.

So how do people find these books?

They search by category on the bookstores and they also use the search bar to try and find something relevant. They type in keywords or keyword phrases into Amazon or Google and see what comes up. **Amazon is a search engine for people who are actively ready to buy**, so you definitely want your book to come up in relevant searches.

Try this.

Go to Amazon and change the search filter to Kindle Store so you are specifically focusing on ebooks.

Now type in 'how to' and see what happens.

You'll get a dropdown of the top search terms that begin with these words.

Type in 'how to market a book.' You should find my book on the first page. The title of that book was designed to help discoverability. I didn't call it something clever. I just titled it with the best search term possible to describe the contents.

I did learn this the hard way, though.

My first book back in 2008 was called *How to Enjoy your Job or Find a New One*. Not the most inspiring title, right! In 2012, after leaving my job, I updated the contents and re-titled the book. It's now *Career Change: Stop Hating your*

Job, Discover what you Really Want to do with your Life and Start Doing It.

The book ranks highly for the search term 'career change', so people find it even though I don't do any marketing for that book and it doesn't relate to my online platform.

Try this search idea for your own topics. It's amazing what people are searching for, and this exercise might give you some more ideas for other books to write.

(4) Write a series and get people hooked

There has been a shift in our consumption culture, in that people are now used to binge watching and reading. They want to watch the whole boxset over a weekend rather than watch one episode a week for months on end. When the latest series of *Game of Thrones* dropped, we watched it over a few days because it's an amazing show and we wanted to immerse ourselves in it. We weren't alone in that binge behavior and the same works for books.

So if you have a series of books and people buy one and they like the characters, they are likely to buy the next one and follow you through the series. This **maximizes your revenue per customer**, whereas if you have standalone books with no related characters, people may read one and then not go back to the rest of your books.

Many authors talk about five in a series being a real tipping point for consistent sales. The aim is to be addictive. Romance authors in particular do this very well. Check out series by Bella Andre, Barbara Freethy and H.M.Ward to see how the real pros do this.

It also works for non-fiction, for example, S.J.Scott has lots of books within the habits niche that each tackle a specific aspect of creating better habits. People who buy one of them are likely to buy more.

You can also **keep promoting the first in the series** to get people hooked in. It doesn't matter if the book was published a while ago because it's always new to someone. Once they discover you, at whatever point in the series, they will likely go back and devour the whole backlist. I'm sure you've done that as a reader yourself. I certainly have.

You can also use a free ebook to introduce people to the series, as I do with *Stone of Fire, ARKANE #1* which is free on all ebook stores. It's a taster that will hopefully pull people in and there are eight other full-priced books for them to move onto.

You can also **write faster if you write a series**. You don't have to reinvent the characters or the world, you just have to come up with a new plot, and that helps add books to the list, resulting in more income.

(5) Think global, digital, mobile and long term

Most authors have a narrow view about where they want to sell their books. They consider the local physical bookstore, or nationwide sales. But the world is changing and, if you own your rights, you can sell your books all over the world.

The biggest market for ebooks is still the US, UK, Canada and Australia but I've now sold books in 84 countries and my books are available for sale in 190 countries. Currently the sales in sub-Saharan Africa, South America and Asia are quite small, but a year ago those sales didn't exist. The rise of the mobile hyper-connected economy means that readers are discovering books through apps. Many of those people don't live near a bookstore, so online retail will be the way they consume entertainment, inspiration and education. Your books can be read by people all over the world – now that's exciting!

So if you're worried about the US ebook market flattening, consider that the rest of the world has barely even started. The next ten years will be extremely exciting for global sales and personally, I expect this to be a greater percentage of my income every year. Make sure you're positioned for this shift.

(6) Write in multiple genres and multiple lengths

Think more widely about what you can write. Don't constrain yourself to just one genre.

This type of silo thinking comes from traditional publishing where authors needed to stay within a brand in order for the marketing team to sell their books more easily into a specific bookstore shelf. But the online sales world is more nuanced, and now there's no limit to what you can do.

Having books in different genres can also hedge against the ups and downs of the book sales roller-coaster. My non-fiction sells better some months, my action adventure other months and crime in the dark months of winter! I fully intend to embrace more genres to continue this spread effect.

I also find it easier to switch between fiction and non-fiction during the day. I can only concentrate on writing fiction for a few hours, so I can then 'cleanse my palate' by writing non-fiction for a while. It uses a different part of my brain and this means that I can write more books over time.

You can also use multiple author names for different genres if you like. This works well if you have diverse audiences. For example, I use J.F.Penn for my thrillers and Joanna Penn for my non-fiction, as the audience crossover is quite small. If you write erotica and children's books, then using different names is also a good idea! But otherwise, there are no rules.

In terms of length, the digital world means readers are less sensitive about shorter works. You won't get a print deal for a novella (around 20,000-40,000 words) but you can definitely sell that as an ebook online. Novellas, or shorter non-fiction books like this one, are easier to consume for readers and offer great value at a cheaper price. They are also much easier and quicker to write.

(7) Consider the up-sell

There is an established price point for books. It's usually anywhere between free and around $100, with most prices hovering at the lower end, under $15. People have been trained to only spend that amount on books, despite the incredible value that's inside.

If you write non-fiction in particular, consider how you could repackage that material into multimedia courses that people are happy to pay more for. People value video and audio more highly than text, so they will pay more for the same information that is packaged in a different form.

Taking this even further, people value personal time and community more than any of these, so if you sell consulting services, events or access, you will be able to upsell even more. I'll go into these options more in Part 2.

(8) Grow your own email list

There are so many options with marketing but the top-selling authors that I know, the ones who are making serious money with their books, only do a few things consistently.

They write a lot of books in popular genres and they grow their own email lists. They offer something enticing for free on their sites and they communicate with readers. They email when books are available and they can chart at the top of the bestseller lists through sales to their fans alongside paid advertising. For more detail on this, check out the webinar replay I did with Nick Stephenson: www.TheCreativePenn.com/nickjo

The tips in this section are all you need if you only want to make money from books. But if you want to take your income into other areas, then read on.

Part 2: How to Make Money in Other Ways

2.1 A business powered by content marketing

This section is all about creating a business online by bringing in multiple streams of income, powered by content marketing.

If we take books out of the equation, what are the other possible income streams from your writing?

Here's just a basic list – then we'll go into these in more detail in the next chapters.

- **Product sales** - Digital e.g. books, online courses. Physical e.g. t-shirts, journals, mugs and other merchandise

- **Service sales** - consulting, coaching, professional speaking, freelance writing, copywriting

- **Advertising or sponsorship** - this can be based on traffic e.g. YouTube videos or by niche e.g. a pet food company sponsoring a pet based blog. This can also include fan sponsorship through Patreon

- **Affiliate income** - ethically selling other people's products or services and taking a percentage of the sale

What is content marketing?

In order to run a business, you need customers to spend money on products or services, which puts money in your pocket and provides value in return.

But how do you get customers to come to you?

With books, the customers are already shopping on the retail stores like Amazon, Kobo and iBooks, so you just have to maximize your chances of being found. If you can write lots of books, that IS your content marketing strategy. Your books are the content that drives people to your other books. But if you're not writing a high volume of books and you want to expand into multiple streams of income, then you have to find some other way to attract customers.

There are many online businesses that power their customer acquisition primarily through paid advertising. I do use some paid ads but mostly, my business is powered by content marketing.

This is the idea of the **author platform**: it's basically a way for you to be able to contact customers, whether by email list, a blog, podcast or subscribers on social media.

* * *

Note: If you need to build your own author website, check out my free video tutorial on how to build your own site in under 30 minutes:

www.TheCreativePenn.com/authorwebsite

* * *

Content marketing is essentially creating quality content that is entertaining, inspirational or educational in order to attract a certain target market. This can be through written articles or blog posts, podcasts, audio, video or images, all of which can utilize your writing skills in various ways.

Remember: There does need to be a point to your content if you want to make money!

Too many writers just throw things up on the internet without having a clear plan for what should happen next.

The aim is that people are attracted to your content and join your email list, subscribe or Follow or Like you or end up buying your books/products/services. It's called the freemium model – you give away quality content for free and people start to know, like and trust you and then eventually they may buy your products or services.

If you have a website, open it up and look at it as if you had arrived for the first time.

Is there a way to subscribe to your email list? Is there a clear enticement to do so, using something of value that the customer actually wants? Is there a Shop or a Books link or a Store or a Buy button? What do you want the customer to do next?

A secondary benefit of an online platform is to build your authority and brand online, which provides other opportunities such as speaking, podcast interviews and being considered a thought leader in your industry.

My site, TheCreativePenn.com, is content marketing aimed at authors and writers. It has:

- Text articles
- Podcast audio interviews with transcripts
- Videos

These are on specific topics relevant to authors, usually educational and inspirational, and provide a lot of value for free. The headlines have been optimized for keywords, making it clear what the content is about.

I started the blog in December 2008 and the podcast in March 2009 and I've been consistent in providing education and inspiration every 2-3 days since then. It's the engine that drives my business and without it, there's no way I could have left my job in 2011 and now be running a multi-six-figure company.

I have something smaller for my fiction site at JFPenn.com, where I write articles and make videos about my research process and also interview other thriller authors. The aim is to connect with other authors but also to provide insight and interesting content for my readers. I've also started www.SupernaturalThrillers.com as a way to build a reader audience around the sub-genre I write in.

It's not all about the money. It can change your life!

A blog, podcast or YouTube channel these days is more like a global publishing platform. It's your way to directly connect with people who love what you do and are interested in your take on the world. This might also be an Instagram account, a Facebook page or any way you have to reach people.

But let's focus on writing since we're writers!

Blogging empowers you because it gives you a way to amplify your voice, to create something new in the world, to change people's lives, to connect with other people and to potentially earn a living.

I absolutely credit my blog at TheCreativePenn.com with changing my life.

It enabled me to **develop my writing voice** – from the corporate form of expression and business writing with no personal touch, to a much more relaxed and open style of communicating through text, video and audio.

I started **selling my professional speaking services** from the blog, as well as my online courses, and it was these things that led to me giving up my job. My book sales were a small percentage of my income at first and have grown over time. I've spoken all over the world, including Bali, Sweden, USA and New Zealand as well as all over the UK, because of my online profile.

My content attracted people who were interested in self-publishing even before the movement became mainstream, and I found **a community of new friends** who have been important on my journey. These friendships enabled me to branch out into fiction, and have directly led to me getting an agent as well as hitting the New York Times and USA Today bestseller lists.

These intangible benefits naturally happen as part of sharing value about your niche online.

Blogging helped me to **develop my position as a thought leader** in the independent author space. Podcasting brought another dimension as I was able to add other people's voices to the mix.

So content is the engine that can drive people to your website, but what do they buy there?

2.2 Product sales

If you have books available through a traditional publisher, or you have self-published, you should have product pages for each of your books with links to all the retailers where they can be purchased. These multiple links are important, because you will find it very difficult to get merchandising from sites like Apple or Kobo if you don't link through to their buy pages.

But books aren't the only things that you can sell to customers. Here are some more options for product sales.

Digital products

Digital products are essentially those that can be downloaded by the customer from a web page, or can be watched/consumed online or delivered by email. They don't need physical shipping or storage, which means that the profit margins are generally much higher than with physical goods. Examples include:

Guides or Resources

If you sell your non-fiction book on Amazon, iBooks, Kobo and the other stores, your price will be dictated by the market, which generally has a cap at around $20 maximum.

Check out any new release from a top author and you'll see this cap applies to even the big names. But you can package your knowledge into a PDF and sell it direct from your website, pricing it much higher than you could on the stores.

Many businesses are selling information this way, calling these Guides or Resources rather than books. The information is the same as a book but in selling direct, you can target your market more specifically and people will be happy to pay more.

Multimedia courses

The last few years have seen a huge growth in MOOCs - massive open online courses. You can find examples at Udemy, Coursera, Teachable, CreativeLive and Masterclass, where I recently did James Patterson's course on story.

The popularity and growth of this 'learning on demand' was demonstrated when LinkedIn bought Lynda.com in April 2015, with the aim of integrating mature, just-in-time career learning into the most powerful professional social network in the world.

You can create your own courses and host them on your own site or use other platforms to host them. I use Teachable.com to host my own courses on writing, publishing and running your business as an author.

Some tips on multimedia courses

I've run a number of courses online over the last few years. Here are some thoughts that may help you if you're considering it:

Do your research into what people actually want and will buy. Don't just create something that you think they will need. If you have an audience already, do a survey and ask people. If you don't, then use Twitter search or other social listening tools to figure out what people want.

Choose the title very carefully. If it resonates, people will buy. This principle is the same for book titles. The language used should be based on the benefits not the features, and the wording should reflect what your target audience are really looking for.

Don't try to cover everything. Keep each piece of audio or video focused on one topic, and don't try to teach everything. Stay hyper-focused.

Sort out your customer service before you sell. One of the reasons why I like writing books is because I'm free to create and put my work out there. There is no customer service except email exchanges with happy readers.

When you create courses, especially from your own site, you will need to interact around technical issues and be more available to answer questions. Make sure that you understand how you will handle all that before you jump in, because you could have a successful launch with thousands of people emailing you for help.

Selling physical products

Unlike digital products, physical products have mass, they take up space and they require physical shipping. But people love them!

The most obvious physical product for writers is the **signed print book**.

Many authors have a separate payment page for signed books and include a link to purchase by PayPal. You'll need to keep a stock in your house and then put them in the mail when you want to send them to customers. Personally, I think that the overhead in terms of time and the very low margin make this more of a marketing activity than a revenue stream but some authors still like to do it.

Many authors also do swag and other merchandise from their websites. You can keep stock and send it yourself, or you can use on-demand services. Comic book artist XKCD has books, t-shirts, stickers and much more at his online store. A simpler example would be David at ThePassive-Voice.com, a great blog that covers the publishing industry. David sells t-shirts with smart indie sayings on his sidebar from Zazzle, which prints the t-shirts on demand.

Selling physical products online is a huge topic, so if it interests you, definitely do your research and due diligence. Personally, I don't sell physical products other than print-on-demand books (yet) so the focus here is more on digital sales.

Payment processing options

It's very easy to take payment online now and you don't need a special bank account setup to do it. Options include:

- PayPal buttons - the simplest solution

- Gumroad, Selz, Payhip or e-Junkie - which have integrated product delivery, social sharing and options to pay with bank cards as well as PayPal

- Woocommerce, Shopify - more extensive shopping carts for use with bigger inventory

There are more options being added all the time.

From my own perspective, I'm now selling courses using Teachable, a hosted service, and Selz to sell ebooks and audio direct to customers from my site.

A short word on European VAT rules instigated on 31 Dec 2014:

Previously, VAT was charged in the country of the seller. Now, if you sell digital products direct to customers residing in EU countries, you are required to pay VAT in the countries where the *customer* resides. Although this was a problem at first, many online retail companies will now handle the VAT portion for you so check with the payment processing solution you are considering to see if it supports this.

2.3 Affiliate income

Affiliate income is commission on sales that you make for someone else's product. There are two main ways in which you can make income with this:

- **Recommend products and services you use personally** and believe are useful to an audience you have already attracted. You can share the information through blog posts, articles, videos and podcasts with affiliate links to the products

- Find products for a niche target audience and then **buy traffic** to send to the product sales page. This doesn't require building up an audience in advance, but it does require extensive knowledge of paid advertising.

The former is a more of a long-term strategy and the one I use personally. I only recommend things that I really think will be useful. However, the paid traffic mechanism can be done in a perfectly ethical way, especially if the product is good quality and useful to the target audience.

How do you become an affiliate?

For many sites and products, you can just set yourself up and you're automatically approved. For example,

- **Amazon Associates** - for pretty much anything sold on Amazon. If you have links to your books on your website (and you should do!), this is a good way to start with affiliate marketing and you will receive a little bit extra if people shop through your link, as well as a percentage of other products that people buy within a 24 hour period. You can use your existing

Amazon account and then find your books, copy the special link and then use that on your site. You can also use a site like Booklinker.net or Books2Read. com to create one link that works for all stores and contains affiliate links.

- **Apple affiliates** - for apps, books, music, etc. sold on iTunes, iBooks and app stores. Again, if you're linking to your books on iBooks, you may as well use an affiliate link.

Many products are invitation-only, based on relationships in the niche that you serve. You are more likely to be approached if you have measurable traffic on a blog, an established podcast, a niche audience that people want to access and/or a substantial email list.

Tips for affiliate sales

Write a blog post or do a podcast or video that outlines the most useful things about the product or service you recommend

For example, I did an interview with Jim Kukral about Author Marketing Club which has a tool that helps authors get book reviews in a more streamlined manner, saving time and energy. It's a useful interview that you can find at www.TheCreativePenn.com/jim

Do a free webinar with the product creator

Webinars are free live web events with replays available afterwards. Make sure to give a lot of great information that the attendees can use to answer a specific problem and then pitch your product with a special deal at the end.

Webinars include video, while teleseminars are audio only. Both options are very popular and generally result in good sales spikes. You can check out a replay of my webinar with Nick Stephenson, where we go into how to automate your author marketing at: www.TheCreativePenn.com/nickjo

Include your affiliate links in your email auto-responder

Your autoresponder is the series of emails that go out to people who subscribe to your website in exchange for something they want. For example, if you sign up to my Author Blueprint at www.TheCreativePenn.com/blueprint you'll get useful emails, articles and videos, some of which contain affiliate links, all for products that I have personally found useful.

Create a video tutorial

Demonstrate how people can use the product you're recommending. One example is my own free video tutorial on how to build your own author website in under 30 minutes which you can find at: www.TheCreativePenn.com/authorwebsite

Create a Tools or Resources page

Include links to everything you use so they can be found in one place. Here's my own tools page as an example: www.TheCreativePenn.com/tools

My overarching tip is to be ethical.

There are plenty of affiliate marketers who don't care about reputation, but for me, trust and reputation is far more important than easy cash.

People *want* to buy things that will help them, or be useful, or entertain them. If we can be trusted advisors who curate a sea of possibilities, then recommending affiliate products is a useful thing to do as well as a great income stream.

2.4 Consulting or coaching

If you are regularly producing content on a topic that educates, inspires or entertains, you will attract people who want to pay for your expertise in person.

One of the easiest ways to make initial income online is to offer your services. You don't need to write a book or learn video and audio skills. You can just put up a page with Hire me, or Book me, or Work with me and then include what you're offering and a button to buy now or directions to PayPal the money to you.

Here are some tips for coaching and consulting services based on my own experience:

Be clear what you're offering

On your sales page, go through what your session will include and how payment works. Is this a one-off session or a series of sessions. How long will each session last? Is it recorded? Are there extra components? What is the rate? Here's an example of a coaching page from my friend Mark McGuinness: www.LateralAction.com/coaching

Include testimonials on your sales page

Work for free with your initial clients and get testimonials from happy customers as social proof that you know what you're talking about. If you offer super value, you'll also get word of mouth referrals over time.

If you're overwhelmed with too much work, put your rates up

I started out with consulting on self-publishing for quite a low hourly rate a few years ago but then it got too busy as my profile grew so I put my rates up over time. I no longer do consulting anymore but this principle is a good way to ensure that you get a high quality of client who is willing to put in the work.

Use a questionnaire and get the client to articulate what they want before the session

After payment, I used to send the client a questionnaire and use that to prep the session. It's important to find out what they want, what their expectations are, and how to provide value, although it's also good to question the assumptions within their request.

Don't be afraid to turn down a client if they don't fit your expertise. Recommend others in the niche who might serve them better instead.

Use Skype to record the call for a value-added experience

I used to do my consulting over video Skype. This brings a personal aspect to the call, and sometimes you need that body language view to really understand what's going on with people. You can also get a real rapport going.

I recommend using eCamm Call Recorder for Mac, which I still use for my podcast interviews, or you can use Pamela for PC to record the call. They are both reasonably priced and you can then send the client a recording of the call afterwards, as well as any extra notes.

What can you offer in terms of a coaching, consulting or other service?

2.5 Professional speaking

If you are regularly producing quality content on a topic that educates, inspires or entertains, you are also likely to get asked to speak.

I made a conscious effort to get into paid professional speaking when I wrote my first non-fiction book and it continues to be an important part of my business. Most of my speaking opportunities come to me now because of my books, blog and podcast.

I know not everyone wants to speak, but if you spend a lot of time writing on your own, it can be a good way to get out of the house and make connections, as well as spread your brand – plus, it can pay very well.

Here are some of my top tips on speaking.

Decide on your target audience and what you will speak about

If you have a book already, the topic will naturally suggest itself and then you can consider the detailed possibilities. You can also decide on your target market and then design a talk or write a book that will appeal to them specifically.

Once you have some key topics, you can adjust your presentation per audience. Although I often speak on the same broad topics, no live presentation is the same, as I am always tweaking the content to make it more specific to those listening.

Call yourself a speaker

Add it to your business card and create a speaking page on your website. It should include what you speak on and how you can be contacted, as well as testimonials and upcoming events. Here's my speaker page as an example: www.TheCreativePenn.com/speaking

Start speaking for free and get some experience as well as some testimonials

You can start small and work up over time. My first speaking event in 2008 was at a writer's group in Brisbane, Australia where I shared my story of self-publishing for the first time.

In 2015, I did the keynote at a publishing conference to a ballroom full of several hundred people, and in October 2016, I spoke on the stage in a full-sized theatre. It just takes time and persistence, as with everything worth doing!

Get paid

If you want to earn money from speaking, then you will need to set your rates after you have been speaking for free for a certain amount of time.

I love sharing my passion but I have learned one important thing: the level of your speaking fee will be determined by the audience you speak for. Clearly, keynoting at corporate conferences on leadership will pay more than talking to a writer's group on self-publishing.

Understand and manage your anxiety

The truth is that pretty much all speakers get nervous in some way, especially if you keep aiming for new experiences that are outside your comfort zone.

For example, I can run a full day workshop with 30 people and not be nervous. I can keynote a conference of several hundred and also be fine. But ask me to read from one of my novels in front of any size of group and I will feel sick with anxiety. I know what anxiety feels like and I accept it. I have my rituals to deal with nerves and you will need to develop them too.

Get some training and join a professional organization if you want to take speaking to a professional level.

Toastmasters is great for learning the basics but if you want to be a paid professional speaker, then check out the National Speakers Association in America, the PSA in the UK or one of the other affiliated organizations from the Global Speakers Federation.

There's a lot more detail about the mindset and practicalities of speaking in my book, *Public Speaking for Authors, Creatives and Other Introverts.*

2.6 Advertising and sponsorship

If you have an audience, people are likely to want to advertise on your site or sponsor your content on an ongoing basis.

Advertising possibilities include:

- **Paid advertising** for a banner ad in the sidebar of your site, a mention in your newsletter or in a video or podcast

- **Paid promotional** article or blog post or video featuring a product or service

- **Advertising on YouTube** - this is more passive advertising in that you turn the ads on and choose when they play, but you don't get to choose the ads themselves

The main thing to remember with advertising is that **you are being paid for access to the community** that you have built up over time. Your audience trust you, so don't do anything to jeopardize that trust.

Over the years, I've been approached by companies offering to pay me a lot of money for leads, but ethically, there is no way I would want to recommend them. In my opinion, your reputation and ethics are more important than money, and you need to respect your audience above all things.

Sponsorship possibilities include:

- **On-going sponsorship from a company,** which implies a longer relationship than one-off advertising. For example, my podcast is sponsored for the hosting and transcription by Kobo Writing Life

- **On-going sponsorship from your community**. This can be the most rewarding as it's actually from your community. My time spent in producing The Creative Penn podcast is sponsored by my listeners on Patreon. You set up a profile and levels of sponsorship – most people pay between $1 and $5 per show – and then the money is collected and sent by PayPal monthly. This is a growing income stream for independent creators as the acceptance of patronage expands.

If you want to earn money with advertising and sponsorship:

Develop a niche audience and have a regular way of communicating with them

This may be a YouTube channel, a text-based blog, a podcast or even a Facebook page, Twitter stream or Instagram channel. Patreon have their own site where you can send out rewards and updates to patrons.

Measure the size of your audience

Have the statistics ready to share with companies who might approach you, or when pitching if you approach them first. This may be Google Analytics for your blog traffic and your hosting company for a podcast, or email list size.

Decide on your rates

It's difficult to know how much you should charge for advertising, but it will be based on how big your audience is as measured by traffic or listens or views, how long the sponsorship is for and your own confidence at asking. There are industry rates listed online which you can use for starters. Increase your rates as your audience grows and don't lock in sponsors for too long.

Only work with companies that fit your audience and that you're happy to endorse

This will protect your reputation and please your audience and also mean that the advertiser may keep paying you for access since the advert will actually work.

This has been a growth revenue stream for me over the last few years as my podcast audience has grown.

2.7 Freelance writing

Freelance writing is essentially writing for hire for other people's websites, magazines, newspapers or books. You're paid for word count and generally you don't own the rights to the finished product.

This kind of writing is an obvious way to earn extra money when you're a writer, but it is non-scalable, and you can only earn that money once.

If you do write freelance, then make sure that you balance your time between writing for others and writing for yourself. Keep focusing on building your own assets, writing your own books and building your own brand.

Here are some tips for freelance writing based on discussions with friends of mine who make decent income from it.

Make a plan

Freelance writing is hard work and if you end up doing the most basic jobs writing for content mills at tiny rates, you will burn out and hate writing.

So **do your research** about the best ways to earn decent money, learn from successful freelancers, **make a plan** and then target the higher paying opportunities. Only apply for the jobs that fit your ideal situation.

Work smarter, not harder

Writing on the more difficult and in-depth topics will earn you more money than just following the muse. Finding a couple of bigger, regular writing clients or contracts will be easier than jumping on lots of individual pieces of work. Listening carefully to what the client wants and then delivering to that sounds obvious, but so many writers don't do this.

Keep track of submissions, invoicing and payment and be clear on your terms and conditions

If you're doing work for lots of clients at the same time, it's really important to check that money has come in when it should and follow up on time if it hasn't.

There are plenty of freelance writers earning excellent money, so don't undervalue your skills

Don't join a race to the bottom, underbidding people on sites like Upwork. Aim to differentiate yourself so you stand for quality and demonstrate that you're worth the money.

Of course, if you're just starting out, you may well have to do some work for free to get those first credits under your belt. Just don't let that period stretch out for too long!

Write on your own blog

Examples of your writing that demonstrate your expertise can attract clients to you, rather than you having to chase them down. You need a professional-looking site that includes information about you personally, your rates and skills.

Relationships are really important.

Think of your connections as social karma, recommend jobs to others and it's likely that you will get recommendations in return.

Further resources

- **71 ways to make money as a freelance writer** - fantastic guide from The Write Life on paying freelance opportunities with specific rates:

  www.TheCreativePenn.com/freelance

- The Write Life: Helping writers create, connect and earn

- Make a living writing - practical help for hungry writers. Run by the fantastic Carol Tice.

2.8 Tips for content marketing

In this section, I've talked about ways to make money by attracting people to you through content marketing – providing education, inspiration or entertainment for free so that people will then go on to buy your books, products and services. You can use your writing as content to attract customers and it costs time, not money.

There are plenty of ways to attract people through paid advertising and I cover that in *How to Market a Book*.

Here are some of my top tips for content marketing in particular, based on the last eight years of blogging, podcasting, doing videos and social media.

Understand the why behind what you're doing

Many people will start a blog, a podcast, a video channel or a social media account and later will question how they can 'monetize' it. If you start by considering the following questions, it will help you later:

- Who do you want to attract?

- How can you educate/inspire/entertain them?

- What do you want them to DO next, for example, subscribe to your email list or buy a product?

- How does this contribute to your income streams or your other definitions of success?

- Is there a point?

Model others

We all start out knowing nothing and we learn from those we find and resonate with. I've modelled my site on specific successful bloggers over the years, as well as emulating authors with incredible businesses in order to shape my own.

So, subscribe to blogs, podcasts or videos that you like, consider why you are attracted to them, work out how the people involved engage an audience and how they make a living, and what you like or dislike about what they do.

Then figure out how it fits with what you're doing. Write your thoughts down and let new ideas spark from there.

If you're serious, own your own site

Many people start out with free websites, like Wordpress. com or Blogger.com but you will soon run into problems with what you can and cannot do.

Also, a free site is ultimately out of your control and can be taken down at any time. The same applies if you build your platform on Facebook or other sites that you don't own. Things can change and you won't be able to do anything about it.

But setting up your own site is easy and cheap these days. Check out my video tutorial with step-by-step notes on how you can build your own site in under 30 minutes: www.TheCreativePenn.com/authorwebsite

Design for mobile and ease of use

Make sure that you use a mobile-optimized theme for your site as Google now penalizes websites in the search engine if they aren't. For ease of scanning, use plenty of white space and sub-headings within your articles.

Build your own email list

Give away something of value that people actually want, whether that's a free book or a video series.

Then communicate to your list regularly with education, inspiration or entertainment that resonates with your brand. If you can build a list of people who open your emails and love hearing from you, then you can definitely make a living this way.

Create excellent content

There's enough crap content on the internet, so make sure your stuff is authentic and real. It doesn't have to be an original topic but it does have to be your take. There are content creators who put out new stuff every day, but there are also people who write big meaty articles sporadically and do very well that way. There are no rules.

Be personal and authentic

Share your personality and your story. More than anything, people crave connection and I've found that the more personal I am, the more my content resonates with people.

From a reader's perspective, over the years I've unsubscribed from blogs and podcasts that have no real personality. The ones I have stayed with, the people whose books I preorder and support, the ones whose podcasts are a must-listen, are the ones I feel that I know. This is the model I try to use myself, sharing my failures as well as successes.

Create focused content within your niche

This may actually fly in the face of the last point! I see it as sharing authentically but within the boundaries of what your audience is there for.

So even though my site, The Creative Penn, really is about me and my journey as a writer, I don't share everything about my life unless it relates in some way to my audience. I keep the site focused on writing, creativity, publishing, book marketing and entrepreneurship, because that's my promise to the audience under that brand.

On my fiction site, JFPenn.com, I *don't* talk about publishing or book marketing because my readers don't care about that stuff. Instead, I share my research for my books and pictures from my travels.

Balance consumption and creation so that you never run out of ideas

When you read a book, take the thoughts you had and write a book review or a lessons learned article based on that experience. Or go to an art gallery and then write something about it.

You need to consume in order to fill the creative well with new ideas, but you also need to create or you will have nothing to sell or share online.

Understand that copywriting is not the same as writing books

If you are a fantastic fiction writer, it doesn't mean that you will be a tremendous blogger straight away. The focus of copywriting is getting people to take action, whereas writing books is usually about the recipient passively consuming. You need to understand the psychology of people's attention, how they scan for what they want, how headlines work and much more. I recommend Copyblogger.com for great info on this.

Link freely to others and share traffic

Generosity and social karma fuel the online world, at least in my experience! It's all about linking to each other within blog posts and social media. This enables stronger connections between peers who may also cite you in return. It also gives you credibility as a good source of curated information. This is essentially how I have used Twitter for years, with a large proportion of my tweets sharing other people's content.

Use images and visual media

It's a busy internet out there with lots of options clamoring for attention but a powerful image can cut through the noise. There are lots of options for royalty-free images and you can also use Canva.com to freely create amazing graphics for your website and social media to make your content more shareable. Videos can take this even further, bringing your words alive with your smile and your personality.

To comment or not to comment?

The number of comments on a post used to be a strong measure of engagement but with the rise of social media, the conversation may happen elsewhere. I am far more likely to share posts and comment via Twitter than on a blog these days. I still have comments on TheCreativePenn. com but I've turned them off on JFPenn.com.

Let it go if it's not working

I've started five different blogs over the last six years and now only retain two of them: TheCreativePenn. com and JFPenn.com, although I have recently started www.SupernaturalThrillers.com as a new experiment.

The others lasted three to six months and I let them go because I ran out of content and I just wasn't passionate enough about the topics to continue writing.

Multiple blogs can take up considerable time, so I only recommend more than one site for regular content if you have clearly defined separate audiences.

Give it time!

I started TheCreativePenn.com in December 2008 and it took about four months of blogging every two days before I saw any traffic or comments, and about six months more before I felt that it was a blog with anything to say.

But in 2010, the site was named one of Problogger's Top 30 Blogs To Watch and then every year since 2012, it has been in the top blogs for writers and self-publishers.

Time in the market and consistency are critical, whether that's writing your books or blogging, videos or podcasting. The longer you commit, the more it compounds and the better the results.

This is just a start, but if you want more on marketing, check out my book on the topic, *How to Market a Book*.

The transition and your next steps

This book has given you lots of options, but now it's your turn. Here are some manageable steps for how you can transition to making a living from your writing.

Remember, you can also use the downloadable Companion Workbook to write down your answers: www.TheCreativePenn.com/makealiving-download

You can also buy a printed version of the Companion Workbook on Amazon and other print bookstores.

(1) Start writing regularly for public consumption

This is not journaling and this is not writing just for the fun of it. This is writing that people actually read.

It could be regular blogging on your own site, posting chapters on Wattpad, guest posting, or writing a book for publication and giving it to an editor.

Set yourself deadlines and then put your writing out into the world, because you have to get used to being read.

Yes, it's scary for all of us. You have to get over that if you want to make a living this way.

By doing this you will prove to yourself that you can write to a schedule, that people will read what you write and that you can take feedback. You will start to grow into your voice, you will relax more about sharing and you'll learn by doing.

(2) Decide what your focus will be and find examples of people to model

Before you jump in, really spend some time considering your definition of success, what you want to create and how you want to make a living with your writing.

Find people who are making an income doing exactly what you want to do and research them even further. I'm just one example but there are lots of others who you can model. There are as many options as there are people! You will find your own models online and many of them will have blogs or will write on forums or answer questions by email.

Read what they've written. Buy their books and courses. Respect their time and only ask intelligent questions after you've been through all of their material.

Curate the opinions you trust with care.

Don't listen to people who are NOT making a living in the way that you want to. For example, an editor working in a publishing house for a fixed salary can't have a true perspective on what it takes to make a living as a creator. They can tell you what their publishing house wants to publish, but they can't advise you on how to jumpstart your podcast audience, or how to sell more books as an indie author.

(3) Prepare something for sale - and then actually sell it

This could be an ebook or a course or selling your own services, anything to prove that you can make some income from your writing. Your first $10 will switch your mindset and will prove you can sell. Once again, you will learn by doing and your confidence will grow because you'll discover that you can earn money in other ways.

Use the options in Part 1 and 2 for ideas as to what you can start with. Then set a deadline by which you will get something up for sale. This is important, since so many people don't achieve what they want because they fail to put a timeline on it. Stretch yourself, cancel other plans and FOCUS.

(4) Grow your audience

Build your email list over time so you have people who are interested in what you're creating. In order to do this, you'll need a professional website and an email capture mechanism like Aweber or Mailchimp. More learning on the job! It's important for your business longevity to have a list of people who are ready to buy. How else will you guarantee your income for the future?

Once you have these basics in place, you're ready to scale.

(5) Grow the number of products you're selling

Once you have proved the concept, you can now expand what you're selling.

This may be more books, courses, audio products or speaking or perhaps adding affiliate sales to the mix. You'll find that once you have made $100 from these methods, you will be able to imagine making $1,000 and then $10,000 in the same way. If you commit to the long term, of course.

(6) Make a plan to switch your income over to writing full time

I don't recommend chucking in your day job tomorrow and attempting to make a living immediately from your writing. It's more of a slow growth curve for most of us.

Start by planning to replace 10% of your monthly income with writing.

Write down what that is for you.

Now do some sums.

If you can make $2 profit from the sale of a self published book, how many books do you need to sell in a month to meet your target? The number might be too high if you only have one book, but what if you have three books or five books?

If you are considering other streams of income, then do the same calculation for that. For example, if you have a podcast that earns you $50 per show in sponsorship, how many episodes would you need to make your income goals? How many listeners do you need to attract that kind of sponsorship?

Once you get to 10%, then you can make a plan as to how to progress. When I reached that point, I made the decision to move to four days a week in my day job so I would be able to take my writing business to the next level. It took me nearly four years working part time to grow my income enough to finally leave the day job in September 2011. Time flies!

(7) Stop procrastinating and take action

I had an email the other day from a lady I met back in Australia. We both did the 'Year of the Novel' course at Queensland Library in Brisbane in 2010. I was working on *Stone of Fire,* titled *Pentecost* at the time, and she was also working on her first novel. In the email, she noted that she was *still* working on that first book, while I was now working on my thirteenth novel. She wondered how I had managed to achieve so much in so little time.

Well, truth be told, there is no secret and we all have the same amount of time.

We get what we focus on.

The difference is that I want this. I'm driven to become a better writer every day, to put out books that will entertain, educate and inspire. I put words on the page every day and commit to this as my career, my hobby, my passion and my life.

If you feel the same way, and you're willing to put in the time, you CAN make a living with your writing.

It's your turn. Now go write!

Need more help?

Remember, you can also use the downloadable Companion Workbook to write down your answers: www.TheCreativePenn.com/makealiving-download

You can also buy a printed version of the Companion Workbook on Amazon and other print bookstores.

If you'd like more help:

- To learn more about becoming a successful author, you can download your free **Author 2.0 Blueprint, plus info-packed monthly newsletters** by signing up at TheCreativePenn.com/blueprint

- If you'd like more detail on **how to run a business as an author,** check out: Business for Authors: How to be an Author Entrepreneur, available in ebook, print and audiobook formats

- **For free weekly audios** on writing, publishing, book marketing and creative entrepreneurship, check out The Creative Penn podcast on iTunes and Stitcher.

- You can also sign up for a free video series, starting with **11 ways to make money as an indie author**: www.TheCreativePenn.com/freedom

You can also tweet me @thecreativepenn or join the Facebook Page www.facebook.com/TheCreativePenn.

Want to take it further?

You know how to write a book.

Now discover how to make a living with your writing.

In the Creative Freedom Course, I share everything I've learned on the journey from first book to making a multi-six figure income from my writing.

Find out more at www.CreativeFreedomCourse.com

Other Books by Joanna Penn

How to Market a Book

Public Speaking for Authors, Creatives
and Other Introverts

Career Change: Stop hating your job, discover what you
really want to do and start doing it!

Business for Authors

How to Make a Living with your Writing

Co-Writing a Book

Successful Self-Publishing

The Successful Author Mindset

ARKANE Thriller series -
writing as J.F.Penn

**Described by readers as
'Dan Brown meets Lara Croft.'**
Available in print, ebook and audio formats
at all online stores.

Stone of Fire #1
Crypt of Bone #2
Ark of Blood #3

The London Psychic Series. Described by readers as 'the love child of Stephen King and PD James.'
Available in ebook, print and audio formats.

Desecration
Delirium
Deviance

A Thousand Fiendish Angels, short stories inspired by Dante's Inferno, on the edge of thriller and the occult.

Risen Gods

You can get a free copy of the bestselling ARKANE thriller, *Day of the Vikings*, when you sign up to join my Reader's Group at:

www.JFPenn.com/freebook

About Joanna Penn

Joanna Penn, writing as J.F.Penn, is a New York Times and USA Today bestselling author of thrillers and dark fiction, as well as writing inspirational non-fiction. Joanna is an international professional speaker and entrepreneur, voted one of The Guardian UK Top 100 Creative Professionals 2013.

Joanna's award-winning site for writers www.TheCreative-Penn.com helps people write, publish and market their books through articles, audio, video and online products as well as live workshops.

Joanna is available internationally for speaking events aimed at writers, authors and entrepreneurs/small businesses: www.TheCreativePenn.com/speaking

Connect with Joanna online:

www.thecreativepenn.com/contact/
(t) twitter.com/thecreativepenn
(f) facebook.com/TheCreativePenn
Google Plus: http://gplus.to/JoannaPenn
www.youtube.com/thecreativepenn

Joanna also has a popular podcast for writers, TheCreativePenn.com/podcasts/

Joanna's fiction site: www.JFPenn.com

More information:

Joanna Penn has a Master's degree in Theology from the University of Oxford, Mansfield College and a Graduate Diploma in Psychology from the University of Auckland, New Zealand. She lives in London, England but spent 11 years living in Australia and New Zealand. Joanna worked for 13 years as an international business consultant within the IT industry but is now a full-time author-entrepreneur. Joanna is a PADI Divemaster and enjoys traveling as often as possible. She is obsessed with religion and psychology and loves to read, drink pinot noir and soak up European culture through art, architecture and food.

Acknowledgements

Thanks to all those who attended my live seminars on *How to Make a Living with your Writing*. Your enthusiastic participation encouraged me to try and encapsulate at least part of the day in this book.

Thanks to Liz Dexter at Libro Editing for line editing, and to Dan Holloway, Clare Lydon and Alexandra Amor for beta reading.

Thanks to Jane Dixon Smith at JD Smith Design for cover design and interior print formatting.

Printed in Poland
by Amazon Fulfillment
Poland Sp. z o.o., Wrocław